MW00638922

The Risk of Sorrow

"The old shall be renewed,
and the new shall be made holy."
— Rabbi Avraham Yitzhak Kook

Copyright © 2014 Valerie Foster and Helen Handler

All rights reserved.

No part of this book may be reproduced or transmitted in any form, or by any means, electronic or mechanical, including photocopy, recording, or any information storage or retrieval system, except for brief passages, without permission in writing from the author or publisher:

Albion-Andalus, Inc.
P. O. Box 19852
Boulder, CO 80308
www.albionandalus.com

Design and layout by Albion-Andalus Books

Cover design by Sari Wisenthal-Shore

Cover photo by Pat Shannahan for *The Arizona Republic* (with an early picture of Helen Handler layered into the background).

Other photos courtesy of Helen Handler, Tom and Valerie Foster.

ISBN-13: 978-0615978222 (Albion-Andalus Books)

ISBN-10: 0615978223

The Risk of Sorrow

Conversations with Holocaust Survivor, Helen Handler

Valerie Foster

with a Foreword & Afterword by

Helen Handler

Albion Andalus
Boulder, Colorado
2014

"To enter into any profound relationship
is to run the risk of sorrow."
— Siddur Hadash
(Helen's prayer book)

Dedicated to the six million
And especially to Helen's family:

Mother, Regina Ackerman
Brother, Nàndor Ackerman
Brother, Miklòs Ackerman
Grandfather, Wilmos Ackerman
Grandmother, Ethel Ackerman
Aunt, Maria Ackerman
Aunt, Berta Ackerman
Aunt, Cili Ackerman

Contents

Acknowledgements

VALERIE WISHES TO THANK Irene Frias, who first set her on the path to teaching Holocaust literature, as well as Kim Klett, David Dummer, and all her fellow teachers who continue to teach the lessons of the Holocaust. She sends out thanks to her student, Richelle Piña, who put her in contact with Mrs. Helen Handler, and to all her students who embraced Helen's words and spirit. She is grateful to Netanel Miles-Yépez, for his shared commitment to preserve testimonies of those survivors before they are gone forever. Her husband, Tom, has earned her undying appreciation for his constant love and patience, as well as thoughtful reading and gentle suggestions. She offers limitless gratitude to Jenna-Marie Warnecke, Emily Groeber, Dr. Billie Cox, and Dr. David Kader, who came to her aide as thoughtful, expert editors. Finally, she thanks Helen "for the love she showed me, the friendship she offered me, the lessons she taught me, and the trust she felt in allowing me to 'peel the layers' of her soul."

HELEN WISHES TO ACKNOWLEDGE her son, Barry, who "gave my life value and a reason to survive," and Rabbi Rick Sherwin, who "watched me go through the sand and come up through the sunshine." She also owes a debt of gratitude to so many, many good friends who, in their own ways, kept her alive, from the concentration camps, to the hospitals, from those in other countries, to those in her Phoenix community today, especially Pat Friedlander, who "gave me love like the daughter I never had." Some friends she knew for a moment, a month, a lifetime, but sees each and every one as "God's way of talking to me."

Preface

GUILTY.

I am guilty. For years, as a high school literature teacher, I avoided material about the Holocaust. It was a topic that had always touched a raw nerve in me that went beyond words. I would rather take my students through Dante's *Inferno,* which I did, than tackle this deeply disturbing subject in a classroom setting. I thought I just couldn't handle it. My students will learn what they need to from someone else, sometime else, I reasoned. There are so many other valuable themes and subjects to tackle, and oh, so little time.

But eventually, another teacher persuaded me to teach Elie Wiesel's *Night,* a little book that opened floodgates of learning for my students and me. We examined the book's literary elements, but even more, we delved into its layered themes on humanity with all its virtues and failings.

I witnessed that magical transformation when literature takes us from the abstract of metaphor to getting to the core message, the heart of a piece. Even a few tall, strapping high school boys, who confessed they'd never read any book in its entirety on their own, were compelled by Wiesel's first words to read every chapter. Indeed, my most resistant learners were moved to new depths of understanding and compassion as they followed young Elie's devastating days in a concentration camp. Elie, fourteen, so close to their own ages.

I realized that there was no more important subject that literature offered us.

This led to my developing a major unit of study for my senior writing classes. We went on to read Viktor Frankl's *Man's Search for Meaning,* performed oral readings of other survivors' journals, and examined relevant films and documentaries.

It is difficult to wrap one's head around the unfathomable statistics of this chapter in history. But learning of one Ann Frank or little Elie brings each of us to a silent communion with another human being. To see high school seniors brought to tears of reverence and empathy, and pour their hearts into essays and discussions to follow, changed my teaching world. I only wished I had had the courage to teach this subject much earlier.

I knew that the greatest impact for my students would be to meet a survivor, and began to wonder if the greater Phoenix area was home to any. Providentially, one of my students informed me that the senior center where she volunteered had just recently hosted a guest speaker, a Holocaust survivor, and perhaps we could have her visit our class. She put me in touch with Helen Handler. I called Helen to invite her to my class; thus began a conversation and friendship of a lifetime.

As Helen reminds me, the whole world is a survivor. Every person has a story to preserve of this historical event, direct or indirect.

Never, *never* forget. The story must go on.

— Valerie Foster

Foreword

THE END OF THE WAR.

It happened so long ago. I felt that I had closed the door on these memories forever. Then a few years ago, with the Solidarity trouble, Poland was back in the news, with the name of a city: Katowice.

To most people, Katowice is only a foreign word, a name, but not to me. For me it brings back dormant memories. All I have to do is close my eyes and there I am once again, walking the streets of Katowice. Before me appear those wide, shaded boulevards framed on both sides by stately, beautiful old homes that tell a tale of past wealth and past culture.

At the end of the boulevard I see a huge, gray, smoky building, the railway station. The station it is crowded; it is noisy. Men, women, and children are speaking in half a dozen different languages, most of the time barely understanding each other.

The year is 1945. A shattered Europe is trying to come to life again. For the last few years Poland was the dumping ground for all human rejects. Now the precious few who stayed alive have to get back…to someone…to their own countries.

In one corner I see a little human bundle sleeping, a girl, still a child. She comes half-awake now and is aware of all the noise and commotion around her. She decides not to open her eyes yet. She's going to play the game, her private little game she used to play in the camp. She used to pretend that she would open her eyes and find herself free again. She had played the game over and over in the last two years. She lost every time. Now the nightmare is over, yet she is still afraid to open her eyes. She is afraid to find herself once more surrounded by barbed wire.

Helen after her liberation.

She wakes up, then remembers that she got in to town the night before. The train broke down. They tell her that there would not be another one going out of here for several days. She accepts this fact without emotion; she is used to accepting facts.

She is told that her journey back home would be delayed for several days. She isn't too upset; she is not in a great hurry. She doesn't bother to explain to them that, to her, home is only a memory. Home is a place where someone is waiting for you. She has no home.

She spends the night sleeping on the cold stone floor, but that is no problem; she has slept in worse places before. She decides to pick herself up and maybe find a Red Cross station with a soup line. She does not rush. True, she is hungry, but hunger is a familiar feeling. Hunger has been her steadiest companion for the last two years.

She tries to rearrange her clothing without much success. She is wearing an old black dress, much too big, way too long for her. Over that, she is wearing an old man's jacket. All of this is not going to place her on the best-dressed list, but she is grateful to have it to keep her warm.

On her head she is wearing an old kerchief tied in a turban. It hides and keeps warm her shaved head. People stare. She meets their surprised looks with complete apathy. Where she comes from, feelings do not exist.

She looks up to the sky; it is heavy with gray clouds. She hopes it is not going to rain. On her feet she wears makeshift slippers made from old rags. They will surely soak through as soon as it rains.

She is amazed to find herself surrounded by a city so busy, so alive. There are housewives hurrying home from shopping, carrying baskets with food—children holding onto their mothers, chattering and laughing—men in the middle of a busy working day, hurrying to their destinations—streetcars and buses filled with people. Somehow she had imagined that when her own world stopped, when her own world died two years ago, the whole world ceased to exist. Yet here it was; it was always here and going on without her all along.

All at once she notices him. He is sitting on the steps in front of a brick building, obviously waiting for a bus. He looks like he is in his mid-teens—so tall, blond, and handsome, so clean and well-dressed.

Judging by the books next to him, he is probably a student.

In his hands he holds a sandwich, two large slices of white bread. It looks like—yes, she is positive—there is butter between the slices. For a moment her eyes are glued on the sandwich. Then she looks up and their eyes meet. Two different worlds: his eyes blue, so full of mischief, so young, so confident; hers dark, so very old, reflecting thousands of years of pain and suffering.

Now he notices her. He is surprised and shocked, but only for a moment. Gradually his whole face lights up with a beautiful, warm smile. He hesitates for a second, then he offers her his sandwich. She doesn't hesitate; she grabs it. She doesn't know any more the meaning of pride. She has learned her lesson well: when someone offers you food, you take it. Don't ask questions—they might change their minds.

She takes a bite from the bread. She doesn't remember ever tasting anything so good. She looks back at him with a smile as she slowly walks away. She decides to eat her bread slowly; she is going to make it last for a long, long time.

This is her first encounter with human kindness and human compassion in the last two years. A faint feeling of hope takes hold of her. She looks up at the sky. Now there is a break in the gray, and there is a little blue showing. The sun even tries to peek through.

For the first time she feels glad to have survived. For the first time she feels that in spite of everything she has seen and lived through, life is still possible.

The War is over.

— Helen Handler

The Promise

"HELLOOOO?" a tiny, feeble voice spoke in a thick Hungarian accent.

"Hello, is this Helen Handler?"

"Yes."

Boom. She entered my life.

"Mrs. Handler, my name is Valerie Foster. I am a teacher at Red Mountain High School in Mesa. My senior writing class has been studying the Holocaust, and one of my students suggested having you visit our class to share your experience with us. Would that be possible?"

"Yes," she responded with no hesitation. "But I will need transportation." Helen, I learned, lived fifty miles away, but I knew I would find a way to make it happen. She was also particular about not addressing too young of an audience, and she was insistent that the students had already studied the Holocaust on some level, so that they brought some semblance of comprehension to her presentation.

I waited for several moments while she checked her calendar. This was already mid-May, with only two weeks left in our school year. As it happened, Mrs. Handler and I could not coordinate our schedules for her to visit, but I vowed to call her the next semester. Our conversation was brief, but something in her voice put me at ease as I tried to picture the woman on the other end of the phone line.

The following fall, my husband, Tom, took the afternoon off from his own faculty position at a nearby community college to drive the hundred-mile round trip to pick up Helen and bring her out to my class. My students were excited and a bit nervous to meet her. The day before they were full of curiosity. "What should we expect, Mrs. Foster?" "How should we treat her?" "Can we ask her anything we want?" These were bright, mature honors students in the twelfth grade, and I did not worry about their behavior. I reassured them that I was sure our guest would answer all questions she could. Privately, I had my own set of anxieties in not knowing what to expect. Will she fall apart? Will my students be traumatized? When she arrived, I stepped out into the hall to lay eyes on a tiny slip of a woman, neatly dressed in a plaid wool blazer, thick turtleneck sweater, and dark slacks, walking with her arm in Tom's for support.

I believe there are moments in life when we instantly know a soul we were always destined to know. I looked into her face and her eyes smiled back at me, and I felt a rush of immediate affection. I knew in an instant that this was a woman I would get to know well. I gave her a gentle hug of welcome. She smiled warmly. Her diminutive countenance belied the powerful words she was about to bestow upon us.

My class held a collective breath as she entered the room, walking slowly and with deliberation. Eyes boring into her, knowing they were observing living history, my seniors sat quietly, waiting for cues from me on how to conduct themselves.

"Class, let's give a Red Mountain welcome to Mrs. Helen Handler."

"Hi." "Hey." "Hello," in quiet unison.

I escorted Helen to the front of the room and set down a bottle of water nearby for her. Tom took a seat in the back. Preferring to stand, using no notes, the little 4'11" lady began.

"I was born in Hungary in 1928."

Not a sound came from my students. I began to wonder if they were even breathing. Helen wove her story seamlessly, as one who had told it many times before. Her voice was feeble and rough. She spoke slowly, carefully forming each word through the filters of her heavy accent. Pausing occasionally to take sips of water, our guest looked around the room to see seventeen- and eighteen-year-old high school seniors sitting still as stones, their eyes riveted on her, their faces revealing horror, grief, empathy, even love. She refrained from exploiting her worst, most sensational experiences in Auschwitz, and instead chose to place emphasis on her inspirational themes of making the most of one's life, of giving back to the world, of loving one's fellow man.

"Why am I here and pushing myself to remember these things which haunt me during the day and during the night for sixty-five years? I'll tell you why I am here: because *you* are the future. You are citizens of this world. This is why I speak, especially to kids. Everything I say has a reason, and I am here for that reason. If you don't walk out of here with a message, then I am only spinning my wheels. You cannot change my past. You cannot heal my pain. All you can do is learn what you must do so the world and your children and your grandchildren do not grow up in a world surrounded by as much hate as we did and which still exists in the world. You live in a country where you have the opportunity to go to school and have a future. You must improve this world. If not, we are destroying each other. And ourselves."

She deftly filled our class hour, leaving time for questions and answering each one patiently, sensitively, and respectfully. I watched from the side of the room and thought how ordinary this extraordinary woman appeared. So tiny, with warm brown eyes and an unassuming pose, she looked like anyone's grandmother. My students returned every one of her kind smiles with their own, looking as if they would take her home with them if they could. At the end of our hour, she had put the class at ease enough that, one by one, my students slowly approached her to take her hand in theirs, sharing comments, gently hugging her. She graciously accepted a bouquet of pink tulips we offered her in thanks, and posed for group photos.

Helen with Valerie's class at Red Mountain High School.

For the next two years, Helen visited my senior classes whenever I asked, sharing with us her extraordinary experience as a witness to and survivor of history's most egregious atrocity. My students always sat mesmerized by her thin, raspy voice as she made her way through her memory box, and her visits predictably ended with hugs, photos, and smiles. "If I don't let them touch me by giving me a hug or shaking my hand, then it's not real," she would say.

When I eventually retired from full-time teaching, I was asked by a former colleague at Red Mountain, Emily Groeber, if I would provide transportation for Helen so that she could continue this tradition in her classes. I was happy to help. On our first trek out to the campus, I mentioned to Helen that retirement now afforded me the luxury of doing more writing. I shared with her that I had written a yet-unpublished personal memoir charting my journey into the dark labyrinth of my daughter's eating disorder. Cars sped past us on the freeway and she listened attentively as I summarized my story. Then she became very quiet for a few moments. Finally she spoke.

"Valerie, you should write my story," she stated. I would soon learn that every sentence from Helen rings as a declaration, if not a command.

"Oh, my. Really?"

"Yes! I would like my story to be written, to be preserved, but I am a speaker, not a writer. Others have asked to write my story, but no one I feel comfortable with. You should do it."

"Well, Helen, I am honored by your offer." But I hesitated, reluctant to commit to such an undertaking. "I will have to think about it."

For the next two weeks, I thought of little else. Here I was being nudged toward a subject I really, really did not want to visit. The very mention of the Holocaust still remained so completely unbearable, so untouchable that, as a defense, I sometimes gave myself the shameful permission to take mental detours whenever the subject rose before me, slipping conveniently into *After all, it's over, can't we just move on* dismissal. Please, please don't make me go there, Helen. Do not make me immerse myself into horrors I cannot undo. And after thirty years of teaching, isn't my service for the good of humanity satisfied? Can't I, now that I have retired, just have it easy? And yet, a strong force pulled within me that here was an extraordinary opportunity being placed in my lap. What else is retirement for, but to be open to new endeavors? I've often found that once one is available, the universe opens up, steps in, and is in your face, as if having simply been waiting to be invited.

Besides, how does one say *no* to a Holocaust survivor?

I decided to meet with Helen to dabble my toes in the waters of this proposed project. No promises, no commitments. Besides, I knew the volatility of the publishing world. I knew that, even if I were to write her story, there were no guarantees of publication. But I also felt within my core that, regardless of our outcome, I would not regret my time with her. Already I could tell this was going to be a profound experience for me and I would be the richer for it.

And so, on a crisp December morning, in freezing rain, I drove the thirty-five miles to Helen's small two-bedroom, second-story condominium in north Phoenix. Walking up the twelve concrete steps to her door, I noticed the menorah on her kitchen windowsill and mezuzah affixed at a slant on her doorframe and knew I was about to enter an environment where I would learn much. The teacher was now the student. Armed with pen, pad, recorder, and trepidation, I knocked softly on her door.

"Good morning, Valerie," Helen smiled at me in greeting. She welcomed me into her modestly decorated living room, with its mural of birds in flight and pink lilies on the wall, and tried to pacify her little Bichon, Pup, who greeted me with hyperactive yapping. "May I pour you some coffee? It's a little chilly this morning."

"Yes, thank you."

Our journey had begun.

While Helen poured us some strong hazelnut coffee, I gazed around her cozy living room, trying to quickly absorb what I could about this woman. Along one wall were bookshelves filled with classics in French, Hebrew and English, from Lowell Thomas to Dickens to Gibran to Taylor Caldwell, to Bennett Cerf. These were mostly titles from her book club, she told me. My hostess guided me over to a glass-enclosed cabinet, which held her many trophies from Toastmasters, as well as awards and plaques for her community work. She pointed out her favorite, a framed copy of a prayer, "Woman of Valor." She told me that in Jewish tradition, a husband recites this at the start of the evening meal at Shabbat to honor his wife. It begins, *An accomplished woman, who can find? Her value is far beyond pearls.* In two minutes I had already had my first lesson. She set down a tray with the coffee, Pup took her place in Helen's lap, and our conversation began to take shape.

It became clear to me early on that this first day's work was a get-to-know-each-other encounter, which is as it should be. This was the honeymoon phase when members must simply sniff around each other like dogs and find one's proper position. Helen seemed very comfortable opening up her life to me. She brought out photos of her father, her husband, herself, and her son, Barry, all in the tradition of portraits taken when everyone is young and vibrant. She told me she has no photos of her mother, nor any other single remnant of her family or childhood. I caught my breath as I was reminded of the story I would inevitably hear.

Not one for small talk, she plunged right into sharing with me various aspects of the Jewish religion and its traditions. As a "raised Catholic" girl, one who has fallen by the wayside of her own religious community of late, I was intrigued to learn more about this perpetually mysterious, ancient community of followers. With each sentence, Helen spoke with great care, precision, and pride.

We sat for two hours enjoying the cranberry/orange bread I had brought, the coffee she'd made, and each other's company. We talked about life in general, about her son, her deceased ex-husband, her health, her seventeen years with Toastmasters, and how she has a girl for my son! When it was time for me to leave, for the sake of her energy and my schedule, she turned apologetic that we had not really begun *the story* yet. I reassured her that this was O.K.; in fact, it was better for us to move slowly. This had been a good day just getting better acquainted with each other. All is well, I told her; we should not rush this process, and it is a process. We agreed to meet every Tuesday from 10 a.m. to noon.

I left that day with my first gifts from Helen: her Jewish bible and a peek inside her home.

All the way home, I felt ambivalence sneaking into my thoughts. *What if I can't do this? What if the subject proves too much for me? What if I let her down? What if this never sees publication? What if, what if?* Yet, before I arrived home, something deep within me told me I would not regret my time with Helen. Already I could tell I was called to do this. I had to move forward. I called Helen the following day and told her that I was making a promise to her to write her story.

Street of the Roses

THE FOLLOWING TUESDAY morning Pup already knew the sound of my arrival. She barked frenetically just hearing my car pull up. I walked up the dozen concrete steps to Helen's door and spied Pup nearly tearing down the sheer curtain at her window.

"Good morning, Helen."

"Good morning. I am so happy to see you back again, that I didn't scare you away," she chuckled.

It was two days before Christmas and before I could even sit down, Helen handed me a gift. I sighed, since I did not have a Chanukah gift for her. She began by saying she didn't know what to get me, then decided she wanted to give me something of hers, "since you are peeling the layers of my soul," she said. Inside a little turquoise and black canvas bag was a cluster of chocolate gold "coins" gathered in gold netting – a Chanukah tradition. Then, wrapped in tissue paper lay a lovely French silk scarf, tan and cream with an aqua flower design and dancing ladies all around its border. I was speechless. She then shared with me the memory of the man who had given her the scarf. He was a renowned environmental architect with whom she had had a decades-long love affair. He wanted to marry her, but she had refused because, while she was a secular Jew, he was from a devout Catholic family, and the inevitable conflict over how to raise children would be too much. He continued to write her once a year until just a year or so ago when the letters stopped. She could only assume that he had died.

I could see in her eyes that just speaking of him elicited in her the sweet, delicious pain of yesterday's love. I held in my hand this beautiful scarf from this beautiful lady telling me this beautiful story and wondered what I was doing there. Why was I being granted entry to all of this?

It wasn't until 11:45 that we got around to buckling down to our task at hand. I turned on the recorder I had brought and knew I needed to take control of this process. I said, "Helen, let's begin with your childhood, to learn about who you were before your Holocaust experience. What is your earliest memory?"

The little woman, sitting in the large Queen Anne's chair, paused for a mere moment and already her expression told me she was now so far from our moment in time and space. When she spoke, it was with slow, measured syllables, coated in a thick Hungarian tongue with rolled Rs and sharp Ts and Ds when she wanted emphasis. At times she struggled to capture just the correct English word or American lingo, mentally translating from any of four languages she spoke, at which I would gently suggest the word. Her voice was soft and she took her time with every breath, with the confidence of one who knows that what she had to say held power and sway over her listener.

"It was a beautiful morning in the fall, my favorite season. I was going through a small gate that led to my grandparents' house. We lived across two alleys that connected. I had a great sense of expectation; this was a special, wonderful day. It was my birthday, September 18, 1933. I was turning five. There on my grandmother's porch were three big packages. Inside one package was a beautiful doll. Oh, she was so beautiful . . . but . . . blonde. I wondered, why was she not darker like me? But she was my new friend, so I decided blonde is good *because* it is different than me. She even wore a dress that matched mine. Later I learned that my three aunts, sisters who all lived with my grandparents, had made my doll's dress to match one of mine. Even at that age, it is family that stands out. My family was all to me.

"The next day, I was supposed to start pre-school. My father took me on the first day. As he and I stood on the school grounds in the middle of a garden of beautiful flowers, all at once my father left and I was alone. Up until this day, I was always used to having family around me. I cried and cried. The teacher ran after Father, who came back and put me on his shoulders. As we went home, a wagon passed by carrying watermelons for sale. He bought one and carried it on one shoulder, me on the other, all the way home."

"What a wonderful image," I said "But that was a rough start! Did you finally adjust to school?"

"Oh yes," she answered, smiling. "In school I had the same teachers as my mother. My mother embroidered a little bag for my lunches, so I always felt my mother was with me. I left home for school each day feeling secure. My teachers loved me. I have a vivid memory of one even putting me on her lap. I felt loved. My favorite teacher we called Auntie Anna. That's how we addressed our teachers, as if they were our family. I went to an all-girls public school in a very good school system. I learned much about America; I knew where New York was, learned about Chicago slaughterhouses, learned about the stock market. But we also learned crochet, embroidery and knitting. We were treated with great dignity and respect. There were not many Jews in my school, but everyone got along. I had good friends. Each Saturday we'd meet in one another's home. We'd eat chocolate and nuts. My teachers loved me and I had friends. I was five years old."

I could see that these early memories were still so vivid and critical in forming this first layer to Helen's life. Her pleasure in recalling them was evident in her smile, as her words were practically tumbling out over each other.

I smiled and said, "Tell me about your family."

"To do that I must first help you understand my land. I lived in a town called Munkacs, in what was originally part of Hungary. For over a thousand years, my land was under Hungarian rule. There are documents to show that as far back as the 1600s, a collection of various Jewry, mostly Hasidic like my family, lived there. In 1920, this became part of the Czech Republic. My family had been in this city for generations. We were a poor community, but we were considered wealthy in culture and education. Jews and non-Jews lived together in peace. So my heritage is one I am very proud of.

"I was born Ilona Ackerman, on September 18, 1928. In Hebrew it's *Szimi*, meaning *fluid silver*. Everyone called me *Simi*. My father's name was Bernhard. My mother was Regina. I had two brothers. My older brother was Nàndor; we called him Nyu-Nyu. My baby brother, five years younger than me, was Miklòs; we called him Mickey.

"I lived on what was called Street of the Roses. It was called this because the streets were lined with cherry trees, and during the months they were in bloom, the whole street on both sides were filled with stunning rose-pink blossoms." At that, Helen's face broke into a broad smile at the memory. "I would wait all year for our Street of the Roses to become a true street of roses. I will never forget that street. To this day, when I want to think of something relaxing to feel safe, I still picture the Street of Roses.

"I remember my father was gone a lot. He traveled all over the country. He owned a hat business with a partner who mostly stayed in Prague. Whenever Father came home, he brought bananas, grapefruit, anything available in the capital cities that weren't plentiful in our town. He once brought a red sweater for my mother. After he died, my mother felt it was not proper for a widowed woman to wear an all-red sweater. She gave it to me when I was a teen. I thought it was beautiful."

Helen was now rapidly weaving together fragmented memories. I sat captivated by the vibrant images.

"I adored my older brother. I wanted to go with him everywhere, and of course he always felt that I was hanging on to him. I was a nuisance to him, like most little sisters. I always said to him, "Nyu-Nyu, please . . ." He was two years older than me and very mischievous. Whenever he got scolded or spanked, I would cry and be angry with my mother. I looked up to him so. One of my most vivid impressions is when my youngest brother was born. I was still five. It was in the summer and so very hot. He had a bassinette that my mother had put in the parlor. She would close the windows and drapes to keep the room cool and dark. I wasn't comfortable in the darkened room, but I felt like the big sister.

"Some of my memories remain very clear. I have detailed memories of going to the synagogue—I keep seeing my father. My mother dressed us up for Sabbath; I remember her nagging which dress I should wear. Oh, I can even see these outfits. One outfit that my older brother and I had matching was a sailor outfit, including a coat with gold buttons. My brother had short pants and I had a skirt. But otherwise it was the same—navy blue. I would be dressed so fine, walking in front of my father to the synagogue. Father was so proud. My mother would stay home with little brother. The synagogue separated the men and women, but I was a little girl, so I could accompany my father. It was always an event of importance.

"In the summer, after synagogue, we would take the long walk home. Father would stop along the way to get a beer. He was not allowed to pay (because it was the Sabbath) but he did, and bought peanuts—*American nuts*, as we called them. We would munch on them all the long way home to dinner."

Helen stopped speaking, lost in a long-ago memory, then got up slowly and walked into her bedroom to retrieve a photo of him. Reminding me that this is the only photo she has of any of her family, it was a formal, full-length shot of him in a fine suit, hat and gloves. "He is dapper, indeed," I remarked, deliberately using the present tense.

Helen's father, Bernhard.

"Oh, yes," she agreed, with a look of pride. "He was a partner in a small factory for men's hats. It was the 1930s and all the men wore hats. He was a good-looking man himself."

"Yes, he was," I smiled. "How did you come by that photograph you have of your father?" I was quickly seeing that our river of conversation would include many tributaries of thought and recollection, which I gladly allowed to flow.

"It is actually an amazing story. After the war, I was recovering in Switzerland and had to remain in bed, never sitting up. For my birthday I got a package from a girlfriend who now lived in New York. I opened it up and there was my father's photograph with a letter describing it. My girlfriend had lived across the street from us. She was three or four years older than I was. We used to talk and dream about our futures for hours and hours. We were best friends. She was Jewish. Her name was Rochelle. We were very close because we shared holidays that other children couldn't understand or share. She was very good to me. She, too, was a Holocaust survivor; she came from another camp. We were reunited when she discovered me in a soup kitchen in Budapest after the war. I was now sixteen and a half, and she was nineteen. And would you believe, she took the initiative to talk to my doctor and learned I had tuberculosis. So she picked me up and took me to the Carpathian Mountains and put me in a sanatorium. She got a job as a nanny for a month or two, not far from where I was, so she could visit me. And then she went to Prague, but still came to visit me bringing clothes her aunts had sent her from America. She brought some of the clothes for me because all I had were pajamas."

I trusted we would chart our way back to the photograph.

"Then she went to New York. Her aunts finally got her papers and she started to work. She wanted to learn English, so she started to take classes in the evening. Her teacher happened to be a Jew whose parents left Belgium before the war, and when she started talking to my friend and found out she was a Holocaust survivor, her parents invited her for a Friday night dinner. While there, they showed her pictures from Belgium, and she said, 'I know this man in this group picture. He looks like my girlfriend's father.' And they said, 'Well yes, he might be because he came from the same town as you did.' They knew my father because he often traveled there for business; in fact, he happened to be there when I was born. So she took that picture to a photographer who took out just my father from the group and sent it to me for a birthday present. New York is a city of millions and every school had English classes. Amazing. Can you imagine?"

Helen gently set the photograph down on her lap. "It is all I have left of my family. I cherish this photograph more than you can know." Her words nearly took my breath away. I thought, *should I pursue this? Should I take this woman by the hand and lead her into deep memories when I know even pleasant ones would lead her to sadness?* Yet, I went on.

"Tell me about your mother."

Helen sat quiet for several moments, as if struggling to find the right words, or deciding whether to speak on this at all. "I don't think my mother ever really felt emotionally the same about me as about my two brothers. She used to say that I wasn't a nice-looking baby when I was born. That I had hair that was growing up to half my . . .," she gestured to her eyes. "And she took honey and bread and put it together to take off that hair so I would have a nice forehead. But my father… my father thought I was the most beautiful child.

"I don't think she ever got over the fact that her husband wasn't there when she gave birth. He was in Belgium on business. But why wasn't he home when I was born? She also got a breast infection when I was newborn and couldn't nurse me. How did my mother feel about a baby who didn't want to take her milk because she had an infection of her breast? I wouldn't touch it."

Helen was now caught in a years-old stream of thought.

"I don't know, maybe all these things kept her from bonding to me. Anyway, I sensed her feelings as I was growing up, and I sometimes blamed my father since he was the one who wasn't there. But after I got married, I knew that it was my mother's fault. Why didn't she go with him? Why did she have to stay home, next door to her parents? Why didn't she grow up and go with her husband? He never wanted to live where he lived. He was someone who wanted to go to Israel; he was a man who was born in the wrong time and the wrong place. He had a very open mind; he wanted to see the world. He always said he had to be away for his business; maybe he wanted to go to get away. He didn't want to be that close with my mother's family; they were visiting our house several nights a week and such."

Keep going, Valerie, I thought. "I know your father died before the war. How did he die?"

Helen again sat silent, her eyes lowering in reverence and reminiscence. When she finally spoke, her words came out with great reluctance, as if with each word she was taking another step back in time.

"I remember a cold Friday in February—a snowy, wet, cold day. A Friday afternoon. We were snowed in. As I sat in the warm kitchen, the house, as always, smelled delicious. My mother was preparing a Shabbat dinner. She wanted it just for us five, no other family. I can still see her standing at our white wood stove as she created this cozy, warm atmosphere. I felt so comfortable. I felt the meaning of a *home*.

"Mother brought in logs which I was to put under the stove nice and neat while she cooked. Brother burst into the house in his winter clothes, blurting, 'My friends told me Father died. I know they're wrong. I'll go fight them after lunch!' My mother ran to my grandmother's house. She came back sobbing. The smell in the kitchen suddenly seemed to sour. I remember how my other brother looked at my mother. 'Say it isn't true!' I couldn't stop crying. In that instant, my home life ended.

"We learned that my father unknowingly had an allergy to shellfish. He did not know this due to his kosher diet. He ate lunch with this in it. His throat swelled. He was rushed in a cab to hospital in Prague where they tried to cut open his throat. He was thirty-four years old." Helen paused, looking as if learning this for the first time herself. "My father was an easy-going, open person who loved life. He didn't worry about money. That's why we didn't have any when he died!" she half-chuckled. "He was a gambler too—he played cards. He'd travel for days for his sales job, and all the salesmen had too much idle time sitting on the trains; there wasn't much else to do. So when he died, Mother cried that we had not a penny. He had no life insurance. My mother had begged my father to get life insurance. He didn't see the value in it. He'd always say, 'Why should I pay all these years?' Oh, the irony of it," Helen sighed. "This was 1935.

"After my father died, his company brought us about twelve suits of his that he kept in Prague. They were from such a good fabric that my mother had them made into suits for my two brothers for the next ten years! Every shirt, every handkerchief was monogrammed by hand. Father was buried in Prague. At that time, children didn't go to funerals. I always felt left out of that good-bye. That was my first idea of what death was, and the first time I lost a home. You know, I am not like him, but the consequences I carry. I am a product of him.

"Immediately after my father died, my mother, brothers and I moved in with my grandparents and aunts. I have often wondered, why didn't my mother open her home to boarders? She was a great cook. She cooked for the whole family, baked for the whole family. You know, there were no kosher restaurants, well, there weren't too many restaurants, period. Remember, this was the 1930s. I believe we could have found a way to stay in our house.

"There were now nine in my remaining family: my mother, two brothers, three aunts, Cecelia, Maria, and Berta, my grandparents, and me. Space was limited. There was never room for me in the kitchen with all the aunts. We also had a maid or two servants in the house. This was not a sign of wealth; it was common then. My aunts had not married because already by then Hungary had joined with Germany, and Jewish men of military age did not go into the army, but were sent to work camps called *Munka Tabor* (Labor Service). Few Jewish men remained in our city to the age of forty. They just disappeared.

"While we lived in my grandparents' house, my mother constantly reminded my brothers and me, 'This is *not* your home. We are here by the goodness of others. Nothing here is ours.' So from age five, I never felt entitled to a thing. To this day, it affects how I live. I am not attached to anything in my home. You see these lovely figurines and furnishings?" she gestured around the room, "I own them, yet they are not mine. I feel no attachment, no ownership in this life. Can you understand that, Valerie?"

"I'm trying to."

"This trauma happened to me at such a young, impressionable age, that I could not reason my way through it; I merely had to accept it. I was dependent on the kindness of others. Or later . . . the savagery."

"I can see that."

"My extended family was very good to us. They loved us. But we never, for one moment, felt that we were home. Which is what every child needs, don't you think?"

"Oh, yes, of course."

"My family was good to me. I was taught to actually kiss my mother's hand every night and thank her for a good day before I went to bed. Every day. And if we had relatives who came to us, we kissed their hands. It was a formal type of relationship. It was such a different time in the world." Helen eyes gazed off in thought. "My grandfather was absolutely my most favorite person in the world. He made a sled for us by hand and would put my younger brother and me in and pull us through the streets in the snow. My grandfather smoked and had asthma; he couldn't breathe. For Shabbat he always had candies for us grandchildren in his suit pockets. They always tasted from cigarettes. He was a very good person. He was the only one who handled us.

"I was a good-looking child, but no one would have ever told me that, to keep me modest. My aunts dressed me like a doll, often in white lace pinafores with little Shirley Temple white socks. I was spoiled. Everyone did everything for me trying to give me a full life. Yes," Helen spoke in a sort of declaration, "in general, my early childhood was a fairy tale." She stopped and leaned forward in her chair. "Until it wasn't."

I felt my muscles tense up, knowing that here is where we pivot.

Helen continued. "My universe began to shift. Our whole city was hit with typhoid. Despite my mother taking all the precautions, Nyu-Nyu still got infected with the fever. He was seventeen. The doctor had to take him away to the hospital, but my mother couldn't go with him because Jews were not allowed to go freely any place they wanted to, and our house was quarantined. That was the first time I saw my mother have a panic attack. I now know what it was because years later when I was in Canada and in the United States, for years I used to have panic attacks. But as a child I didn't know what was going on. I watched my mother shake out of control. How horrible for my mother that they took my brother when he was so sick. I felt so helpless. And then, one evening we opened the door and there was my brother standing there and my mother, who had had no communication with him for weeks, knowing that he was so ill, fainted. We asked if he'd run away, he said no, they just told him that he was all right and that he should go home. Just imagine, after having been so ill he had to walk from the other side of town and no one ever notified us of anything! He didn't matter! How could you let a child go out at night after he had typhoid and say, 'O.K. you can go' and then push him out? And I don't even remember if he found his way home right away. It was dark outside and there he stood. I think my mother thought she saw a ghost. From then on my mother was always worried about us."

I could see our time was up for the day. Helen's posture seemed a bit lower than when I had arrived, and I worried that this project might be asking too much of her. But as I gathered my things, she walked over to her calendar and wrote *Val* in next Tuesday's space.

That day, I left Helen's with chocolate coins, a small tote bag, a cherished scarf, and a love story.

The following week, Helen had to postpone our appointment due to a medical procedure she'd had scheduled long before. "Well," she said, "I've waited eighty years, I guess I can wait another week." Again, I was reminded how much she has wanted, needed to tell her story.

Arrival in Auschwitz

Many mornings Helen greeted me in her pink chenille zip-up robe and pink slippers, her naturally wavy, finger-combed hair still damp from her shower. At first I'd wondered if I had awakened her. But I knew she always walked Pup early in the morning, so it occurred to me that she must feel quite at ease with me to greet me this way. I took this as sign of acceptance and a privilege. I had the feeling that she was like me; only to my good friends would I appear this way. Since she's letting her hair down emotionally, there was no point in putting on airs. It pleased me.

Little Pup soon developed an innate dog-sense when I was coming. Helen regularly swore to me that she never announced my inevitable arrival, but Pup would sit at the front window for an hour, seeming to know to expect something on those mornings. The little Bichon expended boundless energy when I came in, running, bouncing, tripping over her own little feet. Each time, Helen would delight in saying, "You see, she thinks you are here for her!"

One day when I arrived, Helen took out a loaf of yummy cinnamon bread for us to enjoy and me to take home, assuring me she had another loaf for herself.

We talked about recent air strikes in Gaza, parenting, the holidays. Finally I turned on the recorder and we got down to business.

"Helen, the last time I visited, you were telling me that, aside from the tragedy of losing your father, you actually had a happy early childhood. Let's look at how and when that, and the world at large, changed drastically."

"For that, I give you another history lesson. In 1939, with Jews making up about a third of the population, Hungarians reclaimed our little town of Munkacs. It was one of the towns in Hungary with a

Jewish majority. This is where the real anti-Semitism began, because by now we were under Nazi influence. What has always amazed me is that the Holocaust did not start in the jungle; it started in Berlin, the backbone of civilization. It wasn't rabbis thrown down the steps in Berlin; it was professors at the university. It wasn't our Torah that was burning at the square—they were burning books! They were burning secular books, medical books, philosophy, art, and music. They were burning the support, what people had come up with from their heads, throughout civilization.

"Overnight, it seemed, my world changed. There was very little food by the time I was ten years old because we were Jewish and we didn't get card rations for bread. They sent all the wheat and the flour for the Nazi soldiers and for the Hungarian soldiers who supported the Nazis, so we were being deprived long before. We had potatoes, a lot of potatoes. And I didn't like potatoes. But in the villages there was enough food. So for a time when things were particularly difficult, my mother sent me to our relatives' house who lived in a nearby village. But I never stopped crying, so they had to bring me back home two days later. I was so homesick, and . . .," she stopped short, "I am still homesick. Many times I still ache like when I was a child. I never got over it. I never had a home. When the Czechs left, we all felt the pressure right away. First, I had to change schools. It felt devastating to me, but that was before this little girl knew what devastation could really be."

I asked, "How did this affect your friendships?"

"I had a very best friend. Her name was Erica. We were inseparable. She was Christian, I was Jewish, but it never mattered. We always went to each other's birthday celebration. She'd come and watch the lighting of Chanukah candles, and I mostly remember her Christmas trees. You see, Christmas trees had Christmas candy, square little candies packed in white lace and colored foil. And they didn't have other types of things on the tree back in those days, except candy, the whole tree. And candles. And her mother had one different color every year. All pink, and the candles were in the same color as the candy foils. Her father was a judge and they were pretty well-to-do. In Europe, it's not in the morning they get their gifts. Hungarians celebrate Christmas the night before, as they sing *Silent Night*, which was originally a German song. They light the tree, open presents and then go to midnight Mass. That is mostly all over Europe. Oh, how I remember the trees, pink and light blue and soft green and red and then back to pink. Well, you didn't have to put away the ornaments because you ate them!" she winked at me.

"Anyway, Erica and I grew up together. We were very good friends. She had a big yard and I had a big yard and we would talk for hours at the fence. By this time we were both nine years old. The Hungarians came in November occupying the Czech part. Suddenly one day she said to me, 'I cannot be your friend anymore.' I came home to my mother and I couldn't believe it. My mother knew why. I didn't. I wanted my mother to go next door and find out what I did wrong. After all, we were going to be friends forever. I never saw my mother so helpless because that was the first shock that her daughter got. I looked at my mother and I said, 'Please go for me!' and she said, 'No, this is how it's going to be.' Then she saw my big eyes, so she put her arms around me, then she sat down and put me on her knee and she said, 'This is only politics. It will change. You will see, it will be still okay.'

"But then the Hungarians came in and my mother made little flags for my coat to change from the Czech red, white, and blue to the Hungarian red, white, and green. I remember we actually went out to welcome the Hungarian troops. Erica went to Hungarian schools, she had Hungarian friends, she knew Hungarian songs. But now I had to switch to a Jewish school when I was still in grade school and I didn't know anyone. The Jewish schools were mostly children from very orthodox families and they couldn't go to school on Sabbath. I did. These were such shabby schools. The building was just something they rented. I didn't fit in there either. I eventually attended a Hungarian middle school because there was no Jewish school for that grade. Surprisingly, I was accepted at first, and I even had a little Hungarian costume, or uniform. They were beautiful. Some had shoes, some had boots, full skirts, apron, red and blue and so on, with a white shirt with puffy sleeves and a vest of red velvet. In their hair, the girls wore a shield—what you call a *vest*—tied in back with ribbons and these shields were decorated with flowers of the Hungarian fields, red poppies and blue wheat-flowers. The boys wore tights, some with white fringe on the ends; it depended on the region or the village they were from. We always knew the Hungarian national costume, so my mother made me one.

"And yet, things soon changed again. The other students were a lower class, yet I remember there were certain things I was not allowed to participate in. There were four other Jewish girls. And we stayed to ourselves. The end of the year we had a huge presentation in gymnastics and the teacher picked other girls, not me, and it broke my heart. But we didn't want to recognize it; we felt if we ignore it then it did not happen. We just accepted everything as a temporary situation. My mother tried to reassure us that all would be normal again.

"We tried to adjust to everything. You know, the insidious nature of these times is that changes went slowly. First we couldn't have this, then we couldn't do that. Mine was a Hungarian school, but only Jews went there. We were told: *there are Hungarians and there are Jews. You are no longer Hungarian; you are a Jew!* Can you imagine? After all the generations of my family being Hungarian. Yes, we were Hungarian, no matter what anyone now told us. I tell you what was happening: We didn't change, yet, to our former friends, we right away became rats, big rats coming out from the depths of the ground. I saw my friend, but we never said a word to each other. To her, I had become a r-r-r-rat!" Helen spewed, rolling her *r* with particular venom.

"My universe began to shrink. It changed slowly until finally one day, just after Passover, an inspector walked into my home and said, 'This is not your house anymore. This is not your city anymore. This is not your country anymore. There is no room for you here. You are not wanted.' Can you imagine? The Jews in my community were city leaders, doctors, lawyers, successful businessmen, some of them middle class and some homeless living off of charity. Overnight, we all became the same. We walked out of beloved homes, holding onto hope that our families would all survive these days. As my mother would tell us, 'As long as the family is together, this might change. Someone in the world will speak out for us.' Where were they? We would walk through the streets that my great-grandparents had walked through freely; now we were made to feel like criminals. This was the city we helped build!" Helen pounded on the arm of her chair. "I knew all the children in the homes, but the doors were now closed, the windows now shut from us.

"So, how did I feel? I lost a whole world! I lost a world where I felt comfortable, a world where I felt loved, a world filled with the hopes and dreams of a teenager. After all, I was just at the age when I was discovering boys and they were discovering me. It was spring, the scent of lilac trees filled the air. Birds were laying their eggs. Flowers bloomed telling God *Thank you for creating us*. But my world ended. Even after I survived, I never was home anywhere in this world."

"Did you talk to your brothers about all of this at the time?" I asked her.

"No. Nor my mother. People never talked to children in those days. When my father died, I went through hell. Nobody bothered to even . . . I was just a child. Do you know, I don't know anything about my mother. I don't know how she met my father, because I was too young to be told. It didn't even cross her mind that I am mature enough to understand anything. I only heard a few things from hearing my aunts talking. In 1930, even in America, a fifteen-year-old was a child. At fifteen, especially for girls, you were a child and had no rights. The adults spoke of what was going on between each other, but not to the children.

"The authorities isolated a few blocks in the middle of the city I lived in, and converted it to a ghetto, where we were relocated for a few weeks. I was allowed to take only some of my clothes, one or two outfits. I learned quickly to do without things. Because this was my city, I knew a lot of people, so there was a certain atmosphere of home, although a crowded one."

"It was your community."

"Yes. I was able to walk around during the day, within our confines. The people whose houses lay within these newly-bordered blocks had to open their homes for us to sleep on their floors. I saw one boy I did not know. I had an immediate crush on him. And he on me,"

She smiled. I said nothing, letting the sweet residue of an adolescent romance leave its look on her face. Finally she said, "I don't even remember his name.

"They concentrated on rounding up all the Jews in the city. Outlying villages were mostly made up of only about ten families. All of the families from these villages were taken to a brick factory where the freight train passed through. We stayed and waited there for several days in barracks amid all the bricks until we were transferred. We were one of the last of the Jewish communities in Europe to be subjected to deportation, well, what we thought was merely deportation. The whole system was run by the Hungarian soldiers. In fact, I did not see a single German Nazi until later on the train. I wasn't scared in the ghetto. I was scared, however, when they transferred us to the brick factory. It was there I began to realize how little power we held. Men had their beards cut off—a disgraceful sign of disrespect for my people. One day, the men were all called out to do push-ups. My seventy-five-year-old grandfather tried to obey, but lost his strength. My sixteen-year-old brother went to his aid, and dragged him inside to spare him further punishment.

"Then one morning all of the so-called soldiers burst into the houses yelling at us to gather only what we could carry. We mostly took food, what little was left by then, having shared with others for these weeks. I also packed a few photographs and my little blue velvet-covered memory book, like a scrapbook—it is still so vivid in my mind—and my favorite outfit for attending synagogue. All of these men in uniforms kept screaming at us, 'Hurry! Hurry! Hurry!' as we ran to stand in place. I can still see in my mind many of these people who were already near starvation, who could barely stand on their own, yet we were all treated like criminals. I remember feeling petrified because my brother was screaming back at them. I was so frightened that they might shoot him with their rifles. But every night my mother would try to soothe my fears, telling my brothers and me that at least we were together, and that everything would be all right," Helen paused. "But it wasn't."

Helen shifted in her chair, as if attaching a date to her memory gave it structure. It went from a filmy image to a fact.

"It was April, 1944."

For a moment, I thought she might not be able to go on, as her entire body stiffened and her eyes narrowed in a fierce pain. Then she spoke.

"When we were going to the train to go to the concentration camps, my brother wasn't with us and I kept on screaming to my mother that we could not go because my brother wasn't here and I was just in a panic. I didn't want to go without my brother, and as we were getting into the cattle car, my mother kept on saying, 'Be quiet, be quiet!' Now I understand that my mother was just hoping that he had run away and that he was hiding somewhere. We were all huddled, thousands of us, and all of a sudden he wasn't with our family of grandparents and aunts. The soldiers were pushing us, yelling, 'There is still room! There is still room!' and I looked around and my brother wasn't with us. 'We cannot go without my brother!' I screamed. It was a chaotic setting.

"My mother knew where we were going, but she hoped he got away, that no one noticed with so many people and soldiers pushing and confusion. All at once, one of the soldiers brought him back. My mother didn't ask questions; she didn't ask where he was or why he came back. It did not matter. She just was disappointed that he was there. We were told we had to go to a working camp. I didn't ask questions. I was fifteen, but I knew no one had protection. The minute we left our own home I realized. Once we left our city to go to the brick factory outside the city, I knew that even the adults have no answers. However, I did know it was because we were Jewish. By that time I accepted everything. By that time I was wearing a yellow star, I had had to change schools, my whole world was shrinking and I knew that we do not have power over our own decisions or lives. We were all taken together.

"The doors shut with a tight thud on my family: my mother, two brothers, three aunts, my grandparents, and me. We were among hundreds of people packed into cattle cars each designed to hold a few animals. We were not animals, but to the Nazis we were—even worse. We were crammed into an unbearably small space; they just kept shoving more people inside. There must have been nearly a hundred people in there! There was not room for us all to sit. Those who were sick or old were given a space on the floor to sit on; the rest of us took turns standing. If someone had to relieve himself, he had to do it right there in a shared bucket. If a woman went into labor, she had to deliver right there. There was no air to breathe. It was crowded with scare. It was crowded with pain. Between wails of terror now and then, the people were silent. But it is a silence that is still deafening in my mind, a silence that screams out to the whole world. The railcar had two small windows, but they were higher than most of us, so we couldn't see out. Of course the stench became unbearable. For what seemed like forever, we traveled in frozen fear. I searched the faces of adults for some reassurance, but there was none to be found. Still, my mind could never have imagined what lay ahead. Those walls were the last of life for so many children who had dreams that they never had a chance to fulfill." Helen paused to take in a long breath. "Finally, after four days and four nights, the train stopped and the cattle car doors opened to the expansive scene of Auschwitz."

Her very uttering of the word for the first time caught my breath. I still didn't want to go there. *Do I really have to go there?* I felt my eyes stinging as I conjured all that my brain contained of the images, terrors, and stories I associated with the name, A-u-s-c-h-w-i-t-z. *Steady,* I told myself, *this is why I am here. Do not, do not give in to your emotions.* I took a slow, deep breath and tried to keep my voice on an even keel.

"What were your first sensations?"

Helen took her own long delay as she drifted off remembering, picturing.

"The day had just started. It was a gray, foggy morning, very early, as the doors opened on the cattle car, and spit out humans. We all poured out, breathing fresh air after four days and four nights. I looked around and it seemed to me that this was not a place that God created. I'd just stepped beyond reality and all I could see for miles and miles and miles was barbed wire. Behind the barbed wires I could see women and they didn't have any hair and my mother was next to me and she told me, 'Don't worry. They are probably in some sort of institution. Maybe they are not all right, mentally. Let's stay together because we don't want to be separated.' Everyone was screaming and herding us. It was a chaotic scene. I was confused; maybe this was a hospital. Other prisoners were shouting at us not to make the soldiers angry, warning some to give their small children to their grandmothers, because of course they knew that was the mother's only chance of survival. They were trying to help us. They knew if we panicked and ran, we would all be shot on the spot. It was so unreal. The males were immediately separated from the females. That was the last time I would see my beloved brothers and grandfather."

Pup jumped out of Helen's lap, I'm sure sensing her rising tension, and went into another room. I was grateful to be using a recorder, because by now my hands were shaking and I could not have written down a word.

Helen continued in focused concentration. "I remember the SS women when they came to count us. Every one of those SS women looked so perfect. Each one was so fresh, with a short-sleeved white blouse and a sweater. We were freezing, but they had sweaters under their jackets. I can still see the deep wine color, with a vest, but not with buttons. And they didn't wear earrings. They never wore black like some of the SS men; they wore green. And you know, they never wore slacks. They wore skirts, pleated culottes, below their knees. And their boots were as high as their culottes, and yes, they were always perfect. Perfect! In contrast, I can understand why the Nazis could look at us as if we were not humans. We emerged from animal-like confinement tired, exhausted, confused, scared, our clothes no good. We looked like homeless people, when, in fact, some of us had come from palaces!"

As Helen went on, her speech became more rapid, more punctuated with hard consonants. I absorbed the tension, but I had made the commitment to myself early on to ask the difficult questions. That is the role of a good student. Be curious. Ask your question. And so, "When you've spoken in class, you've mentioned Joseph Mengele." Even uttering his name was difficult for me, second only to Hitler. Mengele, notorious physician, infamous for his unspeakable cruelty through torture and medical experimentation on Jews in the concentration camps, had exposed to the world new depths of man's inhumanity to man. "Was he actually standing there himself?"

"Yes," Helen replied, bluntly. "He was there for the Hungarian Jews. It was 1944, and he was there. As we approached a kind of a hill, or more of a small mound, on top of it stood a very tall, elegant SS officer. This was actually the first time that I saw SS soldiers because back in Hungary it was the Hungarian soldiers who took care of these horrible things. He stood there fresh, starting a new day. This, we later learned, was Dr. Joseph Mengele. Everything on him, his uniform, was perfect. Because I was so short I actually could see his shiny, shiny black boots that I will never forget. Oh, how my eyes were mesmerized by those shiny boots! He looked so perfect, his uniform. He actually had a smile on his face, perhaps to avoid panic. But it is an image I will carry for the rest of my life. Yes, yes, I do remember him.

"As we were separated, men and women, we were lined up five in a line, five in the front, five behind it and so on. We were hurried to walk quickly. What wasn't easy was that my grandmother, who wasn't in the best of health anymore, was next to my mother. Mother tried to help her but…everyone was silent at this moment."

Helen's face began to take on a different look. Her brows narrowed, her mouth tightened, lips pursed, looking as if she wanted to spit.

She continued. "Mengele stood there like God and I somehow knew that this was his world and he *was* God in this world because he just nonchalantly pointed with his riding stick to the LEFT or to the RIGHT. It is no wonder they called him the Angel of Death; he personally chose who would live and who would die. 'Let my family keep together!' were the last words I heard my mother speak. Instead, Mengele pulled me out by pointing at me alone between all six of us, the closest women of my life – my three aunts, my grandmother, my mother and me. They went to the Left. I went to the Right.

"One minute I was with my loving family of women, and the next I found myself alone in Auschwitz. I was fifteen."

For a moment, neither of us knew where to go next in our conversation. I felt a sudden cold pallor wash over me. *Can we stop here? At least for today? Maybe if we stop, we can change what happened next.* No. But my mind needed to process where we now were in her tale, and I had to do this outside of our setting. I told her we were finished for that day. She could see my agitation and offered me a lemon drop candy.

"Here, Valerie, take several of these home with you. They are very good."

"Thank you."

She sent me home that day with bagels, lemon candies, and an overwhelming need to hug my children.

Encampment

VERY QUICKLY, Helen and I settled into a comfortable routine. She would open her door with a smile, I'd come in to greet Pup going berserk at my arrival, and we'd all migrate to the cozy living room. I'd sit at the end of her mauve floral sofa, she in her winged-back matching chair with a plaid afghan draped over the back. Pup would jump from her lap to next to me on the sofa. I'd bring out my writer's paraphernalia while she'd adjust her hearing aid. That is where the common thread of our visits ended, for every day was different in her mood, in our topics, and in my inner resolve. As Helen would often tell me, she is a complicated person with a complicated story. Beyond her smile at the door, I was never sure how she would be feeling that day.

The next time I saw Helen, our visit was quite contentious. Helen seemed touched off by so many things in her week. At one point in our morning, I mentioned having used, among many other resources, the HBO documentary, *Paperclips*, in my Holocaust literary studies. When she heard this, I thought she would explode. "Yes, I've seen it!" she growled, then vented in anger for several minutes on how offensive she found it that these school children were collecting six million paperclips to represent the loss of Jews in the Holocaust. She found it trivializing and unforgiveable, in a sense reducing each life to that of a paperclip. "Why didn't they collect dollars, raise six million *dollars* to send to the poor children of Darfur?" She then railed against even Holocaust museums and the money spent on them that could go to current human rights issues.

"But Helen," I tiptoed, "you, yourself, do what you do out of the need for remembrance, that we must continue to teach, enlighten and never forget. That is what museums do."

"True, true," she conceded.

But she could not calm herself. For the next hour, our conversation remained fragmented. Helen kept distracting herself with Pup; I found myself doodling on my pad of paper. She asked me about my family. I asked if she was following some local elections. Finally, I knew we wouldn't be making much progress that morning and I found myself saying, "I am sorry I upset you. I think I'll go now."

Then, just that quickly, her sails were lowered and she smiled back at me, saying, "Valerie, I think we are close enough now that you should bring me back in when I get out too far. Tell me when I am out there drifting in my emotions."

Now standing at the door to leave, I answered, "But I feel that part of my role here, part of my reparation, if you will, is to be an ear for you. To listen to all you have to say. It is very hard for me to tell you what to talk or not talk about."

"Don't worry; I can take it." Helen half-smiled, as if to say, *my dear, we've only just begun.*

I walked to my car with the candied cranberries she insisted I take, put my recorder and notebook on the front seat, and drove home.

We didn't get to any recording that day.

The next Tuesday morning, as I drove the thirty-plus miles to Helen's home, I worried that I would upset her, or me, or simply fail at my task. I put on classical music in the car and tried to mentally transport myself to a place of peace and resolution.

When I got to her home, Helen opened her door and I immediately felt reassured that she was not still disturbed by the week before. She looked lovely that day, dressed all in amethyst. I found myself subconsciously assessing her each week; she seemed to vary greatly in her appearance, countenance, and demeanor. Yet despite any mood she was in, she always greeted me with a smile. And a hug. Pup seemed to mirror whatever mood she was in. Helen laughed to see her pant and snort and gasp and drool in excitement, always adding on cue, "She thinks you are here to see her!" On that day, Pup was more buoyant than I had ever seen her, if that was possible. "She really loves you." That seemed to be Helen's favorite line each week.

She told me how she looks forward to my weekly visit. What

surprised me was that I did, too. I truly enjoyed being with her. We were fast becoming close friends. When I asked how her week had gone, she answered, “My week? It was good. But yesterday, well, I almost called you and told you not to come. You know, you have never seen me . . . well . . . sometimes I get depressed. But having you here is good for me. You bring me strength.”

She decided to make coffee. Shuffling around very slowly in her tiny kitchen, she measured spoons of hazelnut coffee from a little brown bag from Sprouts, then paused. “Now, was that two I just counted?” “Yes, that was two,” I confirmed. She ran the tap to make hot water to warm our mugs. We always had a little something to nibble on, maybe cinnamon buns or scones, shortbread cookies, or on that day —pumpkin bread I that had brought. She carefully folded two large napkins and set them and our treats on a blue lacquer tray. I carried the tray, she carried the mugs, as we settled into our assigned seats. I turned on the recorder and we began.

“Helen, the last time we spoke, you were telling me about your dark morning’s arrival at Auschwitz. You went one direction and your family another. Did you know right away what happened to them?”

“I didn’t think about it. The minute I was separated I never looked back. I realized *I am alone.* Suddenly, nothing else existed. Again I am being screamed at, *Hurry! Hurry!* I just knew that if I wanted to live it depended on me. No one in my family can help me now. I knew that my mother, my grandfather, no one in my family could help me and I had to cope with everything as it happened. I switched to another world.

“I found out later that my Aunt Marcsu (Marie), who was a nurse, didn’t want to leave her patients because they were all old and sick. When we arrived in Auschwitz, one of the prisoners who helped us getting off the train told her, ‘Go back to your family and we will take the older people. We will take the older people,’ because they knew since she was young she might survive. But she said, ‘But they are so scared. I cannot leave them.’ So she went into the gas chamber with all these old people. If she had listened to them, then she might have lived because they needed nurses and doctors.”

“I’m so sorry, Helen. It pains my heart so to hear of such sacrifice.

What an extraordinary gesture."

"Yes."

"What happened to you next?"

"We immediately were ordered to walk from Auschwitz to Birkenau, a very long distance on foot. Our long walk between the railroad ties began."

"Were you calm?"

"I believe I was numb. There's a difference. It was quite a change in Birkenau, because in Auschwitz the barracks were still made out of brick. In Birkenau everything was from wood. I still had my clothes on from home and we entered a huge room and they told us to strip naked and walk into a very large room. What was horrible to me was that people whom I knew from my home, like my teachers, my neighbors, people whom I was taught to respect, all at once they were standing in front of me naked.

"Some women had their periods running down their legs, and I felt embarrassed for them. SS soldiers just walked between us like we weren't even human. They didn't even really see us. They pushed me down into a chair and started to cut and then shave my head. This was the first time I connected back to my mother. I had had long braids, like Judy Garland in *The Wizard of Oz.* I always wanted short hair, but it was my mother's pride and joy. She used to set me down on a stool every morning before I went to school and brush my hair until it was shiny. Then she took an iron and ironed the bow I had worn the day before so it should be crisp. And this was the way she sent me off to school each day. I hated long hair. But she just loved it so much. So this was the moment that I thought that maybe it's good that she's not here because it would break her heart to watch my hair being shaved off."

"How did that moment not completely destroy your mind?"

"You know, Valerie, when people ask me how I survived in Auschwitz, it's so hard for me to explain that I totally detached myself from the regular world. When I read about multiple personalities in a person, I wonder if I became one, because every morning and every evening, I told myself, *Simi, you're still here. You can take it.* Instead of saying, *I can't stand the hunger, I'm cold, the lice are eating me up,* I told myself to think that *I took today, so I'll be able to take anything tomorrow. This is where I am and I am just going to go on. It's not beyond me to live another day and another day. I can take it; it's not that bad.* Of course, the reality was that it *was* that bad, it *was* beyond imagination, it *was* the horror of horrors, but the mind is sometimes stronger than physical reality. My mind tried to alter my reality. It is what I had to tell myself in order to keep breathing. I didn't think about the future. And that was one of the things that saved me.

"I don't know where this came from in me. I always said my mother did not raise me to survive in Auschwitz. I was never taught that you have to stand up, that you fight for life. I was taught that I was a victim, an orphan. But my circumstances now taught me that you have to fight for your life every day. You do not wait. You do not procrastinate. I want to live now, this hour and the next, and this day and the next day. And I am going to make it. I am going to find a way to make it. And someone will always be there to help me make it and someone always was. And so, everything around me became part of what I have to live now. I disconnected for over a year. The only thing I connected to was hunger. Deep, penetrating hunger. That was always present because there was never enough . . . to really . . . it's not because that there wasn't enough to fill my desire for food, but because there wasn't even enough food. Not even once to satisfy. Not because the hunger was so big, but because physically there wasn't enough food for one meal. It was always present, my constant companion. Not once was my belly satisfied."

I unconsciously set down my pastry.

"Anyway, there is a day that stands out in my memory that can show you how this disconnection served me. I was one of five people chosen from a group to be punished, I don't even remember for what, and for twenty hours I had to stand on a stool that was about two feet tall. No arms. Just a stool with three or four legs. I had to stand on it without food or going to the bathroom or sitting down. It started to rain and if one of the five of us fell off, someone came and put us back on. But I never fell off, because in my mind I blacked out. I didn't exist anymore. I can't remember how I lived through it because my mind totally closed."

I said, "I've read that children of abuse are often able to survive only by mentally, psychologically, and emotionally disconnecting. The mind offers them an escape. It is a survival technique, yet it must lead these victims to disconnecting in other parts of their lives. When you would mentally disconnect, did you go to an ideal place in your mind or did you go to a non-place, a blank, numb place? Did you picture better things or did you shut down?"

"I didn't work at it. It happened automatically. It's not like I went into a trance. I think it was my brain's defense. And I don't know when I developed it, but it isn't like I put myself into that situation."

"So you weren't picturing a better setting?"

"No, I wasn't. I found myself in that situation one hundred percent."

"Was it as if you were out of your body, in a nothing place, mentally?"

"I switched channels. My body automatically defended itself, in my mind, mostly. I didn't prepare myself to get into it. It's really just like switching channels."

"But in that channel you switched to, was it like you weren't there?" I asked.

She nodded. "I was there. It's like having another personality. It's not like I didn't know who I am, but it is that I automatically knew how to survive in *this* situation."

"So you sort of go through the motions of what you have to do."

"Yes," Helen said. "I was able to cope with the situation, but I wouldn't have if I had carried all my baggage into it. So it's not like I didn't know about it, but I didn't think about the bad; I thought about survival. You have to also remember that my father died when I was six and a half years old and everyone was so busy with that situation, and no one ever sat down and talked to me about that. So I learned to take in everything that was happening around me and cope with it."

I nodded. "So perhaps either it was simply in you, or that experience was a providential preparation for later."

"This is true. I think I disconnected for more than a year; otherwise I couldn't have survived."

Helen took a bite of her pumpkin bread. Her speaking slowed. "Never before or since, have I believed so strongly in God, because it was all I had. It was all. I couldn't believe in compassion. I couldn't believe in love. I couldn't believe in justice. None of these things could protect me. I must believe in God. Maybe He would . . ." her voice trailed off.

I tried to bring her back. "When I've seen footage of Auschwitz, I am struck by how huge it is. Huge!"

"Well, Auschwitz had A, B, C and then it had Birkenau. People who came first to Auschwitz worked because they built these barracks; all of these two camps were built by prisoners. Yes, the barracks were huge because there were a thousand women in one barrack. There were bunk beds, top, middle and bottom; they were as long as one person and ten people were on each bunk bed. That means there were thirty on each bunk going around against the wall. In the middle there was a place for the prisoner who was put in charge of overseeing us; she was older and had been there longer than anyone, two or three years already. So now she was a guard. These were the capos."

"Oh, yes, we've talked about these in class. The capos were fellow Jews assigned to guard the rest of you. That really pitted victim against victim, didn't it?"

"Yes." Helen's lips locked together in bitterness.

"They were spared, not just from more brutal treatment, but their very lives, and even granted privileges of various kinds. It seems they really had little choice, though." Even as I said this, I braced myself for her reaction to my mitigating the circumstances.

"Well, I don't know," Helen said in irritation. "I do know that it was its own form of psychological cruelty for both the capos and us. I still remember ours because she was so well-dressed. She wore a jacket and on the jacket was a big red stripe with paint. She even had a pleated skirt and stockings. She had shoes and she had hair. She had hair." Helen stopped, as if to let the significance of that simple fact leave its impact. "And she used to walk up and down with a baton to beat us. When she said, 'You have to get up!' you had to get up. 'Schnell, schnell, schnell.' *Quick, quick, quick.* The SS people called us *schwine-hund*, which means 'pork dog.' *Schwine* is *pork*, but when you tell your children, 'You eat like a little pork,' in English there is no degrading word for pork. In German, that is degrading. It is considered a low form of life.

"The first people who came to Auschwitz had striped clothes. We didn't. We just had the junk they didn't want to send to Germany. They gave me some old clothes, not my clothes. So now I didn't even have a thread that tied me to my past, to my home. So I stepped out of that world and out of who I was. I got some underwear that, of course, didn't fit me; it was way too large. The dress I was given must have been for a pregnant woman. It was very cold in Auschwitz in April and I got a summer dress. I still remember how it looked. It had stripes going from the top to the bottom, one white stripe going up from top to down, and one stripe going top to down in a royal blue. On these stripes on my dress, the white stripe had blue dots and the blue stripe had white dots. The bottom, since I was so short, reached to my ankles. It was huge on me. It was a summer fabric, not a soft fabric. It was a hard fabric I could tear off from the bottom a little bit. I had to make a decision. If I tore off a half foot, no, not even that much, about five inches, then I could put a ribbon around my shaved head that was very cold. I shouldn't tear more because I didn't have any socks, so my legs were also cold. Every inch of fabric became so valuable."

Helen leaned close to me and said, "Do you know, Valerie, this still affected me many years later. I had a drapery store in Phoenix. Salespeople used to leave me sample books that I could order from. Every day I received notice from sales reps telling me which books were now discontinued. But I never threw them out. I had three employees, and when I was away, even for an hour for lunch from my store, they said, 'Let's hurry. Helen is not here,' and threw out some of those books that we could not use anyway. But for me, every scrap, every inch has value. I have now, in plastic bags, underwear that I will never use, but I never throw them out. I have a friend who comes sometimes and goes through my drawers and my closet asking me, 'Do you ever wear this?' All I say is, 'No' and close my eyes. And she throws it out. I don't accept that it's happening; I ignore it. I always tell her and I always told my employees, that you shouldn't throw it out; you could find someone who might want it. To this day, I cannot throw out anything edible or usable."

"This summer dress you were given, was this all you were given to wear?"

"I had that same dress until I left Auschwitz. My underwear held up because I had no soap or water so I only washed one thing at a time in cold water. They had huge basins outside with faucets and we could wash our clothes there."

I was bursting with questions, the questions of one whose own life seemed from another planet. "How would you describe your average day? Were you assigned to labor?"

"At Auschwitz and Birkenau I did not work. It is from there they selected transports to go out. In the mornings, I washed as best I could with cold water, then I stood in line for hours for food. I sometimes walked around a bit. We could not spend time inside the barracks. We had to be outside. Even when it rained we had to be outside. I spent a lot of time listening to the women as they talked about recipes. They got together a group of four or five and they would plan a big celebration dinner for liberation and everyone decided they would bring something and everyone had to say how they cooked what they brought. So that's how they exchanged recipes. Fantastical feasts. They created banquets when there were as many as ten women. It gave them strength because in their world, women didn't have jobs. So when they did cook all these special delicacies that's what they cooked for their families. It gave them purpose in their minds."

"You said the women were separated from the men. Did you have only female guards?"

"No. We had both."

"But you didn't see any male prisoners all that time?"

"No I didn't. But I did see male prisoners in Stutthof."

"Were there frictions between prisoners or were they kept close enough to starving that they didn't have the energy to not get along? Were there issues, arguments, squabbles . . .?"

"Never! This is what is unbelievable. When you see fighting in regular prisons, they can squabble because they have food; it's lousy food, but it's food. There was never anger."

"Because you are at that most base level of human needs."

"Yes, yes. Everyone had to concentrate on staying alive. But it also had to do with our background and the Bible; *we must be the light for all nations.* In that inhumane environment, we never became inhuman or lost our humanity."

I put my pen down and took a sip of my now tepid coffee, glanced at my watch realizing how much time had flown by that morning. I had been avoiding one question for some time, but knew I'd have to ask it at some point. I breathed in slowly while trying to simultaneously sound casual. "Helen, I hesitate to ask you this, but were you ever subjected to any of Dr. Mengele's experimentations?" *Please God, please say no.*

"No."

Exhale.

"Luckily, he was looking for twins that day. Also, people always ask me, was I raped? My son once told me, 'Mom, I never dared to ask you that.' The truth is, I was so eaten up by lice; I was smelly and I had so many problems between rashes and so many open wounds in my body full of lice that I would have considered it a compliment if someone would have wanted me for rape. As an American, you think that the most horrible thing that could happen to a woman is to be raped; well, that's not so. The most horrible thing to happen to a woman is that no one would, even in their nightmares, want to touch her.

I suddenly realized my mouth was agape. *Close jaw, Valerie.*

"Students also ask me if I was angry at the SS when I was there. Did I hate them when they were standing in front of me? I tell them, 'No, I wasn't. I didn't. That would have taken too much energy.'"

"How did you and others feel about the capos? Were they more loathed, more feared, was there some sympathy for them, did you get to know them?"

"Some of the capos were . . . cruel. They had power, and power can make a person cruel. I particularly remember one capo. His name was Max. He used to pour cold water on us when it was freezing out. Most of the capos were men. They were not armed, but they had sticks. I can tell you that they felt they paid the price for that role because they had been there several years already. I didn't hate them. I envied them that they had warm clothes, they had their hair when we didn't. I knew they had more food. You know I didn't hate anyone in the war. I was too scared of them to hate. I was a child and they had power. You see what I mean? I didn't have time! If I were twenty years old I would have known how to hate. But little children who grew up in a more or less decent family have not learned this.

Helen looked out across her room in reflection. "Growing up, I had never experienced hate. There were people I envied. I used to envy girls who would go to the tennis courts, in their white little skirts. By the time I was eleven or twelve, I was just beginning to find my place in society. I was starting a social life. Where our house was there were a lot of military stations and then they had one big club in the middle of a park where every Sunday I used to walk by the officers' club and there was music and they used to dance. And the parents would sit at the tables. None of them was Jewish. But I used to know some of the girls who were dancing there, if by nothing else, by their reputations. They were pretty girls; they had beautiful hair and beautiful clothes. I remember their clothes. This was in the 1930s, when girls wore a lot of flowered dresses, like in the old movies. And I used to dream about having these things when I grew up. But I didn't quite understand the situation I was in. I didn't see where I fit in. So I knew envy. I did not know hate."

Helen took in a deep breath. I let my imagination paint an image of Helen as a young girl, full of all the hopes and dreams of any other. I thought of the many high school girls I had taught and wondered how many of them would have been interchangeable in her time. Then I asked her how she had maintained her health during these long, long months.

"Considering it all, I was very lucky. We never had soap or warm water or a change of clothes. So, very quickly after arriving at the camps, we had lice. So we were always trying to de-lice ourselves. That took a long time. There were so many you could catch them. You killed them between your two nails."

"Were there other young teens your age?"

"In Auschwitz there were. But we didn't really form bonds. I talked to people, but close friendships could not be formed. Again, this would have required energy that would have to be pulled away from our focus on survival."

Helen suddenly sat back in her chair, looking very, very tired. We had covered quite a bit that morning. I was worried about taxing her beyond her limit. But then she leaned forward again, fervor in her eyes. I knew there was something she must say.

"You see, Valerie, not all Holocaust survivors were in the situation as people were in death camps—not working camps, DEATH camps. And both of the camps I was in were death camps. The whole world is a Holocaust survivor, but not of Auschwitz or Stutthof. I once listened in Israel to a man talking about the Lithuanian Jews who went to Stutthof, as the Hungarians went to Auschwitz. He said he never met anyone who survived Stutthof. So I walked over to him and I said, 'Well you just met one.' I don't even know if he believed me.

"The fact is, the crematorium was only fully functioning the last year. They only came up with it, maybe 1943. Auschwitz was the first camp that had gas chambers. That was the Final Solution. In 1944 when the Hungarian Jews went in, they already had gas chambers because to shoot people is very hard . . . and expensive. Even now, the people in the Middle East who tie a bomb around their body they kill ten, twenty, maybe thirty. But in a gas chamber they could put a thousand to death very quickly. That's how many they put in each time —a thousand! Men, women, little children. The Final Solution. They finally came up with something. So that's why not all camps had gas chambers and that's why Auschwitz became so known because that was the first one to use the gas chamber. Even the second camp where I was, Stutthof, had the gas chamber, but there were other camps that had no gas chambers. The fact of the Holocaust is that only Jews were gassed. We were the only ones who were gassed. Homosexuals were not gassed. Gassing was a humiliation saved for Jews. Many Holocaust victims died of starvation, they died of sicknesses. But they did hang the Russian soldiers and in the morning when we woke up we used to see them hanging."

After several seconds of silence in the room, I realized that I had been staring at the floor, lost in my own visions, and my breathing had momentarily stopped. I looked up to see Helens eyes burrowing into mine. Then she hung her head for several moments. Finally, she looked up to me and solemnly spoke. "So you see, Valerie, when people say 'Put it behind you,' I was still a kid."

"You were forming your world view by this."

"Yes. Exactly. I remember sitting on my bunk bed and it was one practically on the side of the room and I could see barbed wires outside through a small window. And I told myself, any minute they could select me and kill me and out there is freedom! It's a world out there! And you know how that felt? Like God forgot this part of the world. The sun came up and the sun went down and God looked down on us with a cool detachment, like an indifferent bystander. Actually I never thought the camp was part of the world that God created. We are outside the world God created. The world is out there; we do not live in it. We do not. It's absolutely amazing. So that is how one's view of the world is forever altered. I knew when I was separated from my family in the camp, that I am on my own and no one will help me and if I am going to survive I have to do it myself. I had guts, but it is not true that I wasn't afraid. I was absolutely petrified."

I found my mind wandering. How does one maintain a constant level of panic? How does one keep breathing, eating, speaking, sleeping, while all the while "petrified?" Do the muscles tense up, never to release? Does the jaw lock into place in rigidity? Does complete fear show in the face or do the eyes just revert to a hard steely gaze?

Helen brought me back out of my imaginings. "I always looked fragile," she was explaining. "I was small. There were always people who felt protective toward me. But you know what? I never played up to it like some women do because I always taught my son there is nothing stronger than a weak woman. What I mean is, a woman, not really weak, but who plays on your sentiment, who plays *I need help*, is the strongest. The funny part was, no one thought that way about me. I might have looked that way, but they knew. So it's really amazing because I really feel God gives this strength to everyone, but they don't trust enough—God and *themselves*—that they can do it. No, not everyone could have survived, especially in Auschwitz. But once you were not selected to the gas chamber, it was up to you to survive. Two thirds of the Jews perished, but one third survived. And you had to be lucky. Some people survived because they ended up in a good working place. No, they didn't have it great, but they had enough food. If they wanted you to work they had to take care of you a little bit. Not like in a concentration camp where the goal was to kill us."

Helen took a long pause as she stroked Pup. She offered me a hard candy, then said, "Struggling to survive is different for each of us. I am reminded of Viktor Frankl's work in logotherapy, which he established after the war. He was a Holocaust survivor himself, you know."

"Oh, yes," I said. "I used to teach Frankl's *Man's Search for Meaning* in my Holocaust literature unit. Pretty heady stuff for high school seniors. One of the common denominators that he found among survivors was their having something to survive for. Sometimes it was a person, but not always. Sometimes it was a goal. And you've been talking about this non-place in your head and now you say you were unaware of a sense of the future. He also made the point that a finite sense of time helps one in enduring the unendurable. If I know I have to stand on this stool, or keep walking, or stay awake, or even stir a pot on the stove for a determined, concrete measure of time, I can do it. When in a situation of the unknown, that large, black expanse of infinite time, the will crumbles more easily. It assumes this is—or may be—forever. To this day I often say I can do anything if I know for how long. During the time when you were in the camps, were you aware of time?"

"After awhile, time did exist, but only from minute to minute. I knew that I had only my breath that I took now. I never lived the evening or the morning; I only lived in that minute, that's all the energy I had. I was only aware to the next meal. But there were some people, women, who did. I was still a kid, but older women planned, 'When I am liberated . . .' The only time was when someone knew when my birthday was. She said, 'Today you are sixteen. What would you want for your birthday?' And I said, 'I would like a whole loaf of bread just for myself. And a hot, hot bath.'"

"So, at some point, you said, you knew your family was gone. How did that shift your resolve to go on?"

"I never accepted it until after liberation. I was told later on that my brother couldn't stand the hunger and just gave up." Helen's speech slowed down. "You know, in Frankl's book, he recounts that everyone in his camp experience, used to keep one or two cigarettes. Sometimes they needed a cigarette so badly they'd exchange their bread, and when someone finally had three cigarettes and smoked all three in the same day, he knew that person had given up. I had a cousin of my mother's that I met after the war and he told me he was together with my brother in the same barrack and that he just gave up." Helen sat in silence for several moments. Finally, she said, "Sometimes I am still angry at my brother." Silence. "I needed him . . . he was not here."

Even as I uttered, "I'm so sorry," I could feel how flat that sounded. Words cannot cover the depth of this. "Your brother giving up may have been you the next day, or me the day before. Helen, how did you place yourself into that category where you were staying alive for something?"

"Well, first of all, Frankl's logotherapy outlines three reasons why people survived. One of them, as you said, was a goal, one was a decision that they should live and the third they remembered the love that they received in the life they'd left behind. And at the beginning, I practiced this without knowing logotherapy. It nourished my soul. Right from the beginning I decided that I want to LIVE. I want to live! My second thing was I *must* live because someone will walk in and say this was a mistake and we can go home. And at home everything is going to be just the way we left it. If I didn't come home, my family, especially my mother, I don't know how she could survive if I didn't make it. So I had to live for her. The third one was that in every minute and in every dream I found myself in my mother's kitchen and I would smell and taste the food she cooked for us. I even remember potatoes —I didn't like potatoes. Where I come from potatoes were such a main thing like rice for the Chinese, but now potatoes became something that if I had a tiny piece of potato in my rotten vegetable soup it made my day."

"Because of its nostalgic property, not its taste. Because it meant home to you."

"Yes. I could remember the taste of the potato and I couldn't remember why I didn't like it. Ever since then, now I like potatoes."

"It's funny how the mind affects everything, even taste."

"Yes, yes. And what's amazing is that even if I don't cook it, I always have potatoes. I have two things in my refrigerator at all times: potatoes and bread. Always potatoes and bread. I will open up the freezer and show you how much bread I have. Needs which are not satisfied. I never have enough appetite to finish a meal in a restaurant, but I will take a half a roll home. But then I will give it to the birds because what I cannot stand is to waste bread. Bread is something we give thanks for, say a prayer over. That it should go into the garbage, disrespecting it, that I cannot stand, because in the camps people sold a diamond for bread. Some people had one hidden in a cavity of their body, but bread had more value; it gave you a few more days of life. After all, you cannot eat a diamond," she faintly smiled. "You know, I probably couldn't have finished that whole loaf of bread if I got it, because if you don't eat for a long time, you cannot eat a lot. But I would never have thrown it away. I accept the fact that I must always have bread in my pantry. I am just telling you, we will never be secure."

When I left that day, Helen sent me home with pastry for Tom.

Our bellies are never empty, I thought. Our feasts are never just in our minds. I used to ask my students if they thought they would be able to survive the situation in which Helen and so many others found themselves. Many admitted they believed they wouldn't. Of course, I was forced to answer this for myself. Could I? Do I have enough strength of spirit, body, mind to endure the tortures of man? Could I stand on a box for twenty hours? Numbers seem concrete, but they are actually so deceivingly abstract. One can say, "twenty hours;" it doesn't take any effort to speak or write the words. But who among us can actually imagine this? Twenty hours! It is like the tossed-about statistic of the six million Jews or the five or six million others lost in the Holocaust. *Better know it for Mr. Pearson's history test tomorrow.* Numbers can trip across our tongues or march across a page with an almost flippant neutrality. Twenty hours of driving is long, twenty hours of your car's tires staying inflated is not. Numbers, even words themselves, are empty without our attaching meaning to them in the context of the human experience. The key to connecting with our real humanity lies, in part, in translating the limited constructs of numbers to the equal reality of an organic experience. Fifteen months in college. Fifteen months in a concentration camp. Could I have existed in that place for that time? And what would be my logotherapy focus to enable me to endure such horrific circumstances? Who or what would I—could I—stay alive for?

As I sat each week and listened to unimaginable details, I dutifully kept my composure, recorded facts, transcribed conversation, drove to our next week's visit, and greeted my friend with *how are you?* Yet, at unexpected moments between Tuesdays, I sometimes found myself staring into space, distracted from a task, or in the dead of night awake in a cold sweat, wondering why I was crying.

Invisibility

HELEN CALLED ME one Saturday afternoon and began to tell me about The Phoenix Holocaust Survivors Association's yearly commemoration of Yom HaShoah, also known worldwide as Holocaust Remembrance Day. Helen has been a major participant in the organization for years, serving as president for a time.

"Every year, as part of this event, we give our Shofar Zakhor award." Helen explained, "The symbol of the Shofar horn blowing the winds of Zakhor, or remembrance, is what teaching is about. So every year we use this opportunity to recognize a local teacher or leader for his or her dedication to keeping the lessons of the Holocaust alive. And," her voice rose in excitement, "I am nominating YOU!"

"Oh my, Helen. I don't know what to say."

"Well, you don't have to say anything."

"But Helen, surely there are more deserving teachers out there who give much more of their time and curriculum to this subject. Some schools even offer entire semester courses on the Holocaust."

"Well, I am nominating you!"

I had such mixed feelings about this. Once again I was transported back to my life-long reticence to "visit" the Holocaust. I'm just a teacher who was talked in to teaching a special little book called *Night* to my seniors. I tried to make the subject even more meaningful by expanding my lesson to include films, and other journals of survivors, and I collaborated with one of our history teachers to design a cross-curricular project. But I still felt far from worthy of such a tribute. There are teachers who create classes and design entire curricula around the Holocaust. Teachers organize and accompany students on European trips to the camps and other World War II sites. Other teachers give up valuable time in their summers to attend workshops and conferences, or visit Holocaust museums. Many exceptional teachers devote a lifetime to the world never forgetting.

Still, a few weeks later, Helen called again and nearly shouted into the phone, "Valerie, you got it!"

"What?"

"You got it!" she nearly shouted into the phone. My mind raced until I realized what she meant. "You got the Shofar Zakhor award! Isn't it amazing?"

"Yes. I am stunned. I don't know what to say. Thank you, Helen. Thank you so much for this."

"I didn't do it. You did! I just let the committee know who you are and what you do. At this afternoon's meeting, when the committee voted, I was so excited I forgot my keys at the Center!" she laughed. "You know," she added, "I was one of the first recipients of this award in Phoenix."

"Oh, I'm not surprised," I said. "Well, Helen, I still feel that other teachers might deserve this more, but I will accept it with grace and humility in honor of all of us."

A few weeks later, I was to be presented the Shofar Zakhor award as part of the Jewish community's solemn event of Yom HaShoah. The day before the ceremony, Helen left a message on my phone telling me to relax when I give my speech, that she will still love me if I make a mistake, ending with, "Words that come from hearts go to hearts." I arrived at Har Zion Congregation synagogue in Scottsdale, along with my husband, Tom, my sister, Marsha, my son, Greg, and Carol Schmidt, a colleague from Red Mountain. I had never received recognition for something so special and it meant a great deal that they would be there for me. It pained me that my mother couldn't attend, as she was now undergoing chemotherapy for acute lymphoma.

The ceremony was one that will never fade in my memory. It began with a solemn processional of Holocaust survivors, each in dignified dress and bearing a commemorative candle, walking in to the pangs of a violin's strings playing the theme from *Schindler's List*. I looked into the eyes of every single small, sad, elderly face as each made his or her way to the front. What were their stories? What horrors did they see? Did they lose their mother, father, husband, baby? Each walked slowly, showing the payment of age and sorrow. Biting back tears, I felt a moment of what I call practical panic; *I can't cry, I can't cry; my contacts will film up and I won't be able to see my speech notes! Then what'll I do? DO NOT CRY. Dig that fingernail into your palm to distract yourself!* I watched to see Helen enter last, a placement of highest respect. She looked so lovely, absolutely regal in her slow but graceful gait. Taking her seat of honor in the front row, prepared to give the closing remarks, she looked over to me and winked. That calmed my nerves a bit, for which I was grateful, because although I speak in front of groups of people every day, five times a day, to do so for a different occasion, especially one as solemn as this, left me full of anxiety. Following inspiring speeches and prayers, Arizona State University law professor and past president of the Holocaust Survivors Association, David Kader, delivered moving words about this year's Shofar Zakor award recipient. *Is that me he's talking about?* I made my way to the podium, accepted the stunning plaque that reverently held an actual sheep's horn, and began, "Guilty. I am guilty . . ."

The next time I visited Helen, I brought her tomatoes and lemons from a farmer's market. She gave me something to read—two articles by two respected rabbis, both of whom addressed issues of how to live the Ten Commandments. She seemed very distressed that morning. No issue immediately arose, but when I asked if I could begin with a question, she rubbed her face with her two hands and said how depressed she gets and how helpful it is for me to direct our talk with questions because she can't focus on anything specific, just her sorrow. I told her we didn't need to go on today, that we could just visit as friends. "No, no," she said, "It's O.K., I need to tell my story."

I was hoping that my question would conjure a less painful memory.

"Helen, what led up to your liberation?"

I was wrong. This proved to bring even more stinging images to the surface of her mind. She settled back into her chair and began stroking Pup.

"The war was in its last few months, and the Wehrmacht were coming back from Russia. They needed military clothes, so they took out a few people from Stutthof to clean the clothes for them. Before we went on a death march, they took us back to the camp because they wanted to get rid of certain clothes; they hoped to take us all the way to Germany and they wanted better clothes." Helen's body seemed to stiffen and her voice became very soft. "Behind each barrack there was a big hill of bodies—dead bodies. Hundreds and hundreds of cadavers in piles littering the yards. All we could see was an arm, a leg, a head. They were just piled up like garbage. I mean, you know, when you see garbage and you see a little bit of this, a little bit of that . . . These were human bodies, once loved and cherished by someone, once held and nourished, giving and taking pleasure and happiness. Now they were all piled up in a heap, like unwanted garbage that no one ever bothered to clean up. There wasn't a single human being left in that whole camp except us. They had had typhoid and no medicine and they caught it from each other."

I watched my friend struggle to form every word. Each syllable of each word was uttered with deliberation and pain, slowly, reverently, as if in prayer. "They all died. All of them. So . . . they just threw them in the back." Even after all these years, her face held a look of incomprehension.

I sat, unable to move, unable to utter a word. Finally, I whispered, "It is unbelievable." Solemnity hung in the air.

"Yes. Unbelievable," she whispered as an *amen*.

She seemed to need to repeat her phrases, as if framing them might make them easier for me to grasp . . . or for her.

"Unbelievable. Behind each barrack were dead bodies as high as the ceiling. You could see only a skull, a foot . . . because they weren't scattered on the floor, they were thrown in one big pile and the pile was as high as the ceiling of the barrack. There wasn't time to burn them. These are very horrible things, you know."

Once again words just seemed to float in the air above us. I fought my tendency to fill these spaces in sound and simply allowed Helen to find her way through this. Her next words ran through me like a bayonet.

". . . and in one of those piles was my aunt. She was taken away to a working camp, but she and others were brought back before the liberation because the people where they worked didn't want them, so they sent them back to the mother camp."

We both sat for what seemed like minutes on end as this interjection sunk in. The room felt still and cold and sad.

"How did you find this out?" I finally asked.

"Because when I was walking to work one day, I was in line between dogs and SS people and I suddenly saw my aunt and I said, 'I am so glad you are alive!' And she said, 'Well, maybe I will make it since I made it till now.' I live with the knowledge that she could have gone to a good working camp, but she never wanted to leave me alone; she felt that she owed that to her sister, that she take care of me. Every time they selected prisoners for working, she changed with someone. Finally, we were separated anyway. I am the one who survived and she did not. With every selection my aunt could have gotten to a better place."

Helen became very still and silent. I knew I could have argued this logic, and wondered if I should let her go on, but I asked, "Which aunt was this?"

She answered, barely above a whisper, "Berta." She then sat for a very long moment, deep in thought. Pup began to fidget in her lap, snapping her back to the present.

"Anyway, the Wehrmacht came in to Stutthof and said they needed one hundred people to repair and clean uniforms that had come from Russia for the Nazis because they were short of uniforms for the army. This was a chance for me to avoid a disastrous end. What the SS men and women did—there was a sidewalk in the middle with space on the right and on the left and they counted one hundred women to stand on the right side. I was not picked. Of course not, I was short, I was skinny, I had no hair, my clothes were in shreds. I looked at those stronger women—not really strong, but better than the ones left behind, so while the SS men and women were standing and flirting, and joking, and laughing I just walked from the left side to the other right side. So now there were one hundred and one. But they never counted it again. In that kind of moment, you do not evaluate the situation, you do not think about it, you act! Because a minute later, it may be too late. And it would have been too late for me, because the people on the left side were frozen on the spot and were most likely eliminated. If the Nazis realized it, they would have beaten me to death!"

Helen abruptly rose from her chair as if to physically leave the anxiety of the memory, and announced that it was a good time for tea. When she returned from the kitchen and sat down again, I tried to find the right words to ask her my next question. I needn't have worried. Helen had survived far more challenging and uncomfortable moments in her life than sitting in her condo being interviewed by Valerie.

"I hope you don't mind this question, but in your child's mind, because you couldn't understand the politics at your age, while in the camps, did you ever think that there must be something wrong with your people that they would be treated this way?"

"Yes, I always thought about that when I looked at a SS woman and she was standing in front of me and flirting with the guys. Why, I was so close to her that I could smell the toothpaste from her mouth when she was laughing. I looked at her and she looked beautiful and I looked horrible, but still I didn't hate her. I didn't go so far. I knew that things are bad, but I was never sorry to be a Jew. That's what kids sometimes ask me. When I looked at her I didn't want to be her. I recognized her authority only."

"Did you feel their hatred?"

"I didn't feel that they hated us; I felt that they didn't see us. I felt they didn't belong in the same world that I was in. I was so scared! I will never forget it. There were some women who were so cruel, as I've said, that they would put you against the wall and hit you so you got once hit here and once hit there on the wall. On one of our earlier death marches, we never had food or water, only snow. At one point, there was finally water, not only snow. It was like a fountain outside and people were lined up for a drink of water. Because I was at the end of the line, I was the last one to get some. It was my turn. But the SS women said, 'Enough! We have to move!' I thought quickly, *I must drink now*. I approached and took two or three swallows of water from my hand. She hit me on my head and it started to bleed and the blood was running down my back under my clothes. And it was so cold it froze on my back against my skin. And yet, I didn't bother hating her. I felt very lost, very scared. I wanted to live. I always wanted to live.

I didn't waste any feelings on anything else. I was too hungry to hate. There was no energy for emotions.

"I remember liking certain people, fellow prisoners. There was a Hungarian girl, I don't know her name, but as long as I live I will never forget her face. She had the most beautiful dark eyes, and a thin face—well everyone had a thin face," Helen half-smiled. "I don't know if she's alive or if she died. But that face. I don't know why that face . . . She wasn't my friend; we just happened to work alongside each other. I thought to myself, *God she is gorgeous*. She was young, a teenager, maybe a little older than me, maybe eighteen or nineteen. I never saw her before or after. She had the most beautifully huge dark eyes, thin face, thin lips. She was probably hungry," she lightly chuckled. She added quietly, as if musing out loud, "I remember that girl's eyes and I still have a dream of her once in a while.

"I had people I liked and I had people who liked me, but I particularly had people who did help me. One of them was able to help me because she slept with a capo. The girls who slept with the capos were really . . . they did not do it by force, they did it for advantages, and the greatest advantage was survival. Who can blame them? Maybe they had a sister there to protect. They did it for surviving. Every person who was generous with me, who passed on some food to me, or whatever, slept with the capo or had a sister who did, so that's how they got more food. And I profited from it. It's the sisters who felt more sorry for them, because the girls who did it, it did something to them. They . . . they became insensitive to what they had to do. You see, in a situation where you have to make a choice, having it easier by screaming and even hitting other people gives you more of a chance of survival. Or even the person I'm talking about who saved two other sisters, she certainly saved me. Actually, her sister saved me."

"What happened?"

"This was near the end. One of my fellow prisoners was a twenty-year-old girl from my city. I didn't know her from home, but we were practically the only two or three left from there. She was very good-looking, even with a shaved head. She was blonde, blue-eyed, she had everything . . ." she seemed to drift off in an image. "She and her three sisters always looked after me. The youngest sister slept with the capos, so she had a lot of protection. One day, a leader from the Wehrmacht needed people to clean and press uniforms. He told the sister, who was sleeping with him, to pick some people. 'I need twenty people,' he said. 'I want to pick my sisters,' she told him, because she knew this would mean getting away from the camps, and certain extermination. He said O.K. So she picked her sisters first. But she couldn't pick all twenty. The opportunity came when they closed the barracks, but for leaving one window unlocked. She was the only one outside, and was calling to us, 'Go to the window. I am going to pull down the three of you.' The window was bigger than we were—we weren't very fat! She was able to open a window and pull out her two sisters. One of the sisters, Anna, who always liked me, put me first so she was sure that I would go. We knew we were soon leaving on a death march, so I knew this was a chance for me to survive. She kept on saying, 'Come! Come!' So they took my hand and we went to that window. One of the sisters pushed me before she went through the window because she knew her sister was not going to leave her, but she might not take the chance of taking me out. Then the three of them went down from the window. A few other people followed. It went so quickly they didn't even know what was happening. So the window was just opened a little bit, in more ways than one!" she smiled. "Other people couldn't jump out on it because it was right away closed again and they would have been shot if they had. So, she saved me. She saved me for another chance to live, and I would like to give her credit. Her name was Ibie. In Hungarian, the *ibola* or *ibie* is a flower, a violet. Her shortened name was Ibie, but her full name was Ibola, or Viola."

Helen looked like she wanted to cry. But she held firm. Then she began to fidget in her chair as if it were suddenly very uncomfortable. "There were many situations like this where only a very few selected people with connections were fortunate enough to get out. One of them was an opera singer with her mother. I remember them because she used to sing arias for us from operas and I don't know if she survived, but she and her mother escaped that way. She used to sing while we were in the camps. The Germans would pick her up to sing for their events."

I noticed that my friend was beginning to calm herself and her face changed to a look of peace. "So, ask me how I survived," she continued. "Unbelievable. There was always someone who protected me. All my life I met someone like you. Out of nowhere. Do you know what I mean?"

"No, what do you mean?"

"If you think about it, Valerie, I could live here in my neighborhood for a hundred years and never meet you. We are not in the same circles; we are not in the same generation. We don't even shop at the same Costco or at the same gas station or at the same Wal-Mart. To me, your neighborhood is another country. And yet, you were put before me. And I have always had someone like you when I most needed it."

When I left that morning, Helen gave me the commemorative candle she had lit at our Yom HaShoah ceremony, a Jewish prayer book, and butterscotch candies.

My ride home did not call for the soothing strains of Mozart or Bach on my car radio. I felt bitter and confused and sad for my friend. Suddenly, so much in the world did not make sense. Helen was guiding me into its madness and we both had to find our way out. Covering the miles of freeway home called for the loud, hard, cacophonous rips of hard rock to drown out that morning's words and images. Led Zeppelin would do.

Liberation

We made quite a pair of unconventional friends, Helen and I. With vast differences in age, background, religion, politics, and whether cinnamon bread should have raisins, we might have had a tough time breaking through barriers to deep affection. Not the case, for we also enjoyed our share of commonalities. At 5'1", I had finally found someone whom I could tower over. She told great Jewish jokes, and I fractured many an Irish one. We both knew the challenges of divorce and single motherhood. And early on, we both revealed that neither go in for small talk. She, because she has too many big topics and time is of the essence when one is eighty and has a very big story to share. Me, because frankly, chit-chat bores me. So we made a good pair.

Often I would arrive home from a "Helen day" to have my husband ask me, "How did it go, hon?" and all I could give in response was a pained expression or a curt "I can't talk about it right now. You have no idea." But my friend and I also shared many moments of tenderness, even laughter. She was taking up permanent residence in my mind during the week and each visit began and ended with a lingering hug, particularly when I'd leave, with her often planting a soft kiss on my cheek.

One morning I showed up wearing a simple, somewhat drab olive green tee shirt. It was, after all, St. Patrick's Day, so being full-blown Irish, I had to wear green. But I didn't want to wear one of my many wild, crazy St. Paddy's Day shirts because I always strove to respect a certain tone to our visits and the inevitably heavy topics our discussions would lead us to. So on that day I kept my *Who's Your Paddy* wardrobe at home. I didn't even mention the holiday.

That night, after arriving home from a friend's party, there was a phone message for me from Helen forging each word with emphasis. "Valerie! I forgot to wish you a Happy St. Patrick's Day. But it is partly your fault! You did not wear gr-r-r-een! I would have remembered if you had worn green, but you wore beige! So, I am sorry I forgot, but it is your fault, too! I hope you had a nice St. Patrick's Day." As I said, Helen is about accountability.

I called her the next day to say thank you, and explained that I had, indeed, worn green. After all, I have an Irish reputation to uphold.

"Well," she retorted, "it did not look green to me!" She went on to tell me that my phone number is right next to her rabbi's and she first called him by mistake. When he answered, she assumed it was Tom, so she lapsed into her long tale about forgetting to wish me a St. Patrick's Day. Boy, was the rabbi confused!

The following week I knocked on her door and as she welcomed me in and I put my arm around her, Pup was performing her usual climb-the-wall sequence. Helen followed with, "She even knows your name now. I tell her, '*Valerie* is coming,' and she runs to the window to wait for you. It is amazing." I handed her a loaf of her favorite cinnamon bread I had brought. "I see you remember I don't like the kind with raisins. This is good. Thank you."

We had a good laugh over the St. Pat's Day blunder. When I asked how she was, her now-standard reply was a slight smile and, "Hanging in there," or "Up and down." Then, before we could complete our slow walk to her living room, she launched into whatever was most on her mind and we hit the ground running. *Keep up, Valerie.*

This day's issue was over a speaker who was going to address educators at an event to be held at the Ina Levine Jewish Center. He was a German Jew whose family had gotten out of Germany before the war broke out. Helen was familiar with his work and knew in advance that his thesis was how basically good the Germans were . . . are. That only twenty percent of them supported Hitler. Helen was near hysteria at this. She felt so insulted by his mitigation of the Germans during World War II, not to mention that she had not been invited as part of the agenda.

"They don't have a single survivor speaking at this teachers' conference. This event is for teachers all over the Valley who teach about the Holocaust. They will take a day off from classes and come to this to receive all sorts of materials and ideas for teaching the

Holocaust. Who can better inspire their work, their extraordinary commitment, than one who was there?" She sat with her back rigid. "Well, I am going to speak, and they can't stop me."

For some reason, I knew I should be there, even if just to help her post bail once she made a scene and got arrested.

When I arrived in the lobby of the hall a few days later, I looked for Helen until I noticed a migration moving toward a tiny figure standing to the side. There was Helen, dressed in a mauve pantsuit, blue crystal dangling earrings, and a touch of rouge, greeting each person with a quiet, unassuming manner and a polite smile. I stood transfixed, as dozens of people made their way over to her to say hello. How is it that the tiniest lady in the crowd can hold such sway? That's Helen. From all her years of speaking in schools, synagogues, churches, universities, and various community events, she can hardly go anywhere without "fans" approaching her in recognition and reverence. I stood from a distance and simply watched the dynamic. *She looks so pleasant, anyone's grand-mama,* I thought to myself, *and always smiling*. None but I knew the secret militant inside who was planning an attack in the name of Truth.

Before the event began, she implored one of the organizers to warn the keynote speaker to temper his speech, then she stood in the back of the room listening as he reiterated his defense of the German citizenry. I could see her familiar look of lips pursed in anger. As the participants broke for lunch, Helen assured me that her resolve to speak had only been reinvigorated. Unwavering in her intent to counter the morning's guest speaker's viewpoint, she got up from the table where we were enjoying a kosher lunch with other teachers, and managed to nudge her way onto the stage while the participants kept eating. She stood behind a podium, mere inches higher than she was, and sought to be heard over the din of teachers eating a free lunch.

"Hello? Hello? Is the mic on? Can you hear me?" Her voice was barely audible. From the back, I could barely make out the little head bobbing just above the lectern. At first she failed to gain much attention. After all, who is this woman? She's not on the program. I felt so uncomfortable for my friend, and wanted to stand up on my Formica lunch table and shout in my experienced teacher-voice, *Hey everyone!*

Quiet! Someone is asking for your attention! Of course, I stayed silent. Better to leave that scene to my imagination. But gradually, lunchers began to look to the source of the sound. Conference coordinators were dumbfounded on what to do, but several knew Mrs. Handler, and knew not to try to stop this diminutive hurricane.

"My name is Helen Handler, and I am an Auschwitz survivor."

At that, teachers stopped talking, forks were set down, and her magic began. She spoke modestly, then vehemently, making her case on accountability. Always mindful of her audience, she concluded with an old Jewish tale: *A renowned rabbi came to visit Jerusalem when it was still a village surrounded by a wall. And the leaders of the village brought out all their most important people to the gates to welcome the rabbi and the rabbi looked around and said, 'Where are the teachers? I want to talk to the teachers.'* He knew that that is where the real influence lies. It is the parents', grandparents', and most of all the teachers' obligation to advance goodness in this world."

Helen ended by telling this group of four hundred educators that teachers always thank her and other survivors who visit their classrooms, but it is the survivors who should thank the teachers for keeping their doors of remembrance open.

"We thank *you*. Without you, our story, humanity's story dies. And it must *never* die. It will survive in our Jewish community, trust me. Our children will know the story. But how will the world know without the teachers? Teachers like you!"

A standing ovation.

Every week I had limited time to visit with her, since I taught class afterward, and often our two hours were largely usurped by us discussing events of her week, or issues in the news. But I always felt that my devotion to her was not limited to recording a story; rather, we had become close friends, and friends listen to each other. There would be time for the Holocaust. She shared her frustrations from the week, her nagging health issues, and fears over world events. Eventually, I brought us back where we had left off. Liberation.

I clicked RECORD on the tape machine.

"Helen, what was the end of the war for you?"

"It was April, 1945. The Germans were losing the war. The Russians were approaching very quickly. So we went on a death march from Stutthof. I'll never forget it. There were times when we slept over in churches because that was the only thing big enough for our numbers. They wouldn't let us out to relieve ourselves, so how do you think that church looked after we left? So that added to their propaganda; they could point to that and say, *see the way these people live—they are sub-human.* And this was in Poland, where they already hated us. But there were some people in certain villages, who lined up along the road and threw food at us, or to us—we weren't quite sure—as they were not allowed to come close to us. It was so very degrading because we would all scramble and fight the others for the scraps. The SS barely organized any rations for us. Sometimes they allowed us to step onto the frozen fields where we would dig out vegetables. We were never given food as we marched. The only food for us was what we had to find for ourselves. In the fields there were frozen beets, no water. We ate snow. Through the night as we marched, we stopped at another camp that was a working camp and they did have much better food and one of the ladies walked up to me and gave me a piece of food that tasted so delicious—I still can taste it—I think it was a piece of fat from a pork. You see, back in Europe in the villages, they ate fats because they needed it due to the weather.

"Our daily fight for survival only mounted on death marches because these treks were really designed to eliminate even more people. If you could not handle its severe demands, if you fell or became sick, or even complained aloud, SS officers would shoot you on the spot. One morning, as we trudged through the cold and snow, a woman dropped down to the ground. I wanted to pick her up, but it was physically impossible. I did not have the strength." Helen stopped and gazed into her coffee cup for a long moment. "I would have to live with that failure for the rest of my life. We all left her there. It was all we could do. I remember the eyes, the eyes, the terror and begging in her eyes . . . and watching her be shot. I always remembered the eyes of people before they died. I will remember her eyes the most. I still cry about it many, many times."

I fought back tears, and sought out Pup to pet.

"On this same death march, I remember vaguely, very vaguely, crossing a body of water in a boat and prisoners were pushing out in line and certain people fell in the water. They never picked them up. They drowned." Helen stopped, in reverence to those who'd perished so cruelly. "Life was so very fragile. Someone living or dying depended on the moods of the SS. We could not be responsible for any one other than ourselves.

"After many days on this death march, I don't know how many, we reached a barn. The SS soldiers didn't know what to do with us. They had become tired of dragging us with them, knowing the Russians were right behind them. The order was that we were not to live, so they thought if they closed us in this barn without food, without water, without going to the bathroom, we would perish. They were almost correct. Several hundred went into the barn. Only thirty survived."

Numbers. Lives.

"I had a kind of a friend; she was there with her mother. I knew her first name—Bobbie, short for Roberta. She was younger, about a year younger than me. Her mother was a beautiful woman. Her father was a very famous surgeon at home. They were very wealthy and she was an only child and she always talked about her piano lessons because she loved the piano. As we were herded into the barn, we tried to stay together, but we got separated somehow. I remember lying there in the middle of the night and hearing her screaming, a voice I will remember for the rest of my life. And she screamed to me in my nickname, 'Ilonka, my mother died!' She didn't know whom to call out to, so she called to me. She knew I might not even be alive at that point; she just had to tell someone that her mother had died next to her. You see, she did have a mother until the last minute, but I didn't. I don't know if she survived. I have no idea. I never met her afterward. Many died on that last day and even after liberation."

"How did you hold on, Helen? How did such a young teenage girl not simply let go to a sweet oblivion of death?"

Helen looked at me as if she had asked this question of herself many, many times.

"You see, when I speak, I mention that God was always my life jacket and even at fifteen, I knew that if I let it go only one minute

I will never be able to get back to it again. It was a full-time job—survival and faith. But even I have my limits, and now in the barn we had no water and no food and my body was being eaten by lice. I had a sweater, it was gray. I can still see it. It was hard as this," as she knocks on the coffee table, "just from the eggs the lice put in it. And I took it off and I was naked and then I noticed my whole body was covered in water blisters. But not just little ones. I had a big one here on my arm," she gestured, "and here and going down my leg and then as I used my elbows and where I was lying, my blister broke and the lice were eating my flesh. And that's when I lost it.

"I don't know how long I was in that barn. I was unconscious when the Russians liberated me. I don't know how I got out of there. What maybe saved me was that they touched me and they knew I was not dead. I still had all these lice on me, but I was probably still warm. I don't remember. But for all these many years, my skin today is thicker, like scar tissue."

On that cue, Helen rolled up her sleeve to show me her arm. I looked at her arms of fair, soft skin with a multitude of tiny scars, and slightly indented pock-marks. My eyes stung.

"Do you know, I can now not wear anything that has a seam because it hurts my skin because of the lice so long ago. So I have to wear something under it and on the wrong side. It's that sensitive. It is so very, very sensitive. Against my body I can only wear the softest cotton t-shirts, usually men's, that have no bulky or harsh seams."

"Dear Helen, your being saved is really quite remarkable."

"I don't know why I was one of the few. I don't know why I was one. Many years later, I wrote a poem addressing one of the many liberators to whom I was so grateful. I want you to read it. I'll get it." She rose slowly from her chair and walked to her bedroom. After a few moments she returned, sat down gingerly, the pride evident in her brown eyes, and handed me a photocopy of her poem.

"I feel it belongs to every liberator."

I read it aloud.

To a Liberator

Did you liberate Paris
Or open the gate to Dachau
Were you welcomed by a victory band
Or met with silence and death
Were you rewarded with kisses by pretty girls
Or did you stare in hopeless empty eyes
Were you soaked in the pride of a conqueror
Or defeated by the shame of humanity
Did you liberate Paris
Or open the gates to Dachau

I looked over to see satisfaction in Helen's face. It was clear this poem was written in great affection and gratitude for those liberators, no matter from where. She shot me a half-smile and told me to keep this copy since she has several.

We both knew our time that morning had ended; I had to teach class in an hour. Before I left, Helen said, "I have something for you." I was getting used to that. She walked slowly into her kitchen to take out a loaf of Passover cake someone had made for her. She cut the loaf to give me half.

I drove the long miles home unable to even listen to my car radio.

Later that afternoon, Tom and I went to see *Valkyrie*, a movie based on the true story of one of fifteen failed plots to assassinate Hitler. It is a tight, fast-paced suspense film, and as the story unfolded, we watched countless German army officers in rebellion against the dictator, racing against time to remove the SS, liberate concentration camps, and restore Germany to its nobility. Suddenly, it was no longer a movie for me, and I found myself weeping, weeping, thinking about how actual brave men risked all, while a little fifteen-year-old girl named Simi waited in a barn. The contrasting backdrop of opulent

Nazi quarters against a barn with hundreds of starving, dying Jews —actors' starched impeccable uniforms against a holey gray sweater made stiff with fleas and encrusted lice eggs—left me sick to my stomach. I was overcome with an urge to stand up, turn, face my fellow moviegoers and shout, "This is not just a movie. It happened!" Instead, I sat huddled, and I wept. And do as I write this.

I knew I would never be the same.

Freedom

A FEW DAYS LATER, a young Jewish boy named Daniel wrote in to the *Jewish News* asking why Jews had not defended themselves against the persecution he had learned about in school. He certainly was not the first to question this. He wrote, "Jews have been persecuted because we were afraid to fight back."

By the time I next saw Helen, she had submitted her response to Daniel, which was printed in the next edition. She handed me a copy. It read:

> *I am weary of being accused, as a Jew in general, and as a Holocaust survivor in particular, of not having courage. What is courage? Does it take courage to burn, to kill, to destroy? Does a gun represent courage? It takes courage to be a fifteen-year-old Jew in Auschwitz. It takes courage to face the gun of an SS soldier, alone, starving, sick, powerless, helpless and in spite of all, hold on to hope and faith . . . and survive. It takes courage to find yourself alone after the war, no home, no country to go back to. It takes courage to build a new life in a new world, learning a new language, adjusting to new customs, becoming a valuable, tax-paying citizen, without expecting help from anyone.*
>
> *Looking back in history, the winds of time have swept away many mighty nations who had the power of the sword. Jews are still here, and are here to stay. For thousands of years Jews had the courage to build and not to destroy. The Holocaust is not the story of victims. It is the story of a people with determination, endurance, perseverance and true human dignity.*

All the Daniels should be proud of their heritage. Their people know the true meaning of courage.

When I looked up from reading, I told Helen how I appreciated this statement, since it addressed an issue many of the rest of us stay silent about. Then it was time to return to where her story took her after liberation.

"It was now 1945. I was sixteen years old. For the world, the war was not quite over, but it was over for me. At the time I was liberated, I was deathly ill, sick with starvation. I was tended to at a makeshift Russian camp. Still in a camp! But at least the food was warm," she offered a weak smile. "Several survivors were foolishly given regular food to combat their starvation, but one of the attending nurses near me knew that this can be very harmful. Many people become very ill, even die, when introduced back to solid and abundant food so suddenly; the body can't take it. So I was given just nourishing liquids, initially. Again, I am being saved.

"But the Russians had to move on. I was taken to a Polish hospital and examined by a French doctor who had been in a camp. He didn't have a stethoscope, but he put his face to my chest and told me in German, 'Say 33,' and decided that I had tuberculosis. At that point I was sent to a sanatorium in Czechoslovakia for six months: Aix-les-Bains. One morning they sent in a doctor to give me a gynecological examination and he could not complete it. A doctor stood practically a half a mile away from me. He never wanted to get close because I had already been determined to have TB. So he walked out, saying, 'I cannot examine her, because she is a virgin.' They just never imagined I was still a virgin having spent time in the camps.

"Next I was sent to a sanatorium in Paris, where it was discovered that my tuberculosis was in my bones, so I was next transported to Lausanne, Switzerland in the Carpathian Mountains to recover and to be treated by a medical professor who was having success in healing bone TB. They placed me on a special mattress where I spent an entire year totally on my back. Can you imagine? I was on my back or on my stomach for more than a year. I never even sat up. I never had a visitor. My care was paid for by an organization of Swiss and American Jews. Now, these were very wealthy people, and they were very generous to sign a check, but no one came to see me. Yes, it was a stunningly beautiful setting. Each room had a balcony with an unbelievably beautiful view, but for me, I could not enjoy it, lying on my back every minute of every day. What I most needed was someone to care about me, a personal touch or a loving word. One of the reasons the hurt never healed was that there was no one to heal it."

"How did you deal with this isolation and loneliness?" I asked her.

"I am still coping with it. When I am alone, my moods are terrible to struggle with. There was a little old lady in my room, another patient, and she spoke only French. I spoke Hungarian and Czech; she spoke neither. But I would talk and talk and talk and cry and cry to her and she would just listen. She couldn't understand a word I said, but she never stopped me. She knew I needed to talk and she listened. When I would sob uncontrollably, she would put her arm around me to comfort me. I will never forget her. I can still see her clearly in my mind. It was an amazing gift for a person to give—the power of caring."

"What true compassion. Would you say this was the period, then, when you could finally react to what had happened? You could give in to the emotions of the experience?"

"Yes. But the real importance of this for me was her humanity. She was old, sick, didn't understand a word, but there was a need and she filled it."

"How did you pass your days through your recovery?"

"Well, they brought in tutors two hours a day and I learned to speak French. Also, I knitted. I set a goal for myself to complete a sweater every month, but of course, by the time I got out, none of them fit me because I couldn't try them on along the way. And so my days went. You see, you cannot rush recovery from tuberculosis. There was no adequate medicine in 1945. Mine was in my spine. The cartilage between two vertebrae was like putty, so the two vertebrae fused together, but the nerves between both did not. It was very painful. They gave me acupuncture that hurt very much. This was sixty years ago; not like today. Needles were bigger and not as refined."

With that, Helen stood up and turned around, pulled her clothes away and underwear down a bit to reveal her lower back. Right in the dip of the middle of her lower back, I could see slightly darker discoloration and a dozen or more little white prick marks to serve as reminders. "I also had spondylitis, which is an inflammation of the lower spine, near my hip, and which still causes me to walk a little lower on one side."

I sat there feeling completely inept. I did not know how to respond to this. I felt an actual physical pain inside, imagining my dear friend suffering. My ever-present attempt to reach for the so-called bright side of things prompted me to settle for a most empty reply. "But . . . you survived." *Oh, Valerie.*

Showing supreme tolerance, she slowly responded in a quiet tone, "Sometimes surviving is not such a bargain."

"Really?" I probed.

Helen looked into my eyes with sobering expression. "Really."

I just didn't know what to say at this point. This woman's life was all about survival. But surviving for what? She survived the Holocaust. But did her spirit? Did her joy for life? Did her appreciation for the company of others? I still threw out a dart for some redeeming point.

"Was there any benefit to this year of 'down time?'"

Helen remained patient with me. "Many of the people who went in to the detention camps in Germany got married and maybe many of them had children there; they started more or less to rejoin life. Well, I didn't. I never rejoined life until 1950 when I left the sanatorium. But even then I didn't because there was no one to learn from. The people who are survivors, some of them were in their 20s when they went to the camps. I was fifteen. I was still forming. There was no grown-up next to me. I was fifteen, thrown into a world that I didn't know—I never had a period of moving gradually from a child to a grown-up. I went from being tended to into a world where I had to fight to survive. It worked two ways—the fact that I was alone was beneficial to me because I didn't have to worry about anyone else. I had lost everything, so all I really had was my life and . . . and maybe the torn up clothes or whatever. In the camps, I didn't even have the luxury to worry about a comb or about a toothbrush or whether I was running out of soap, things that even in a jail people normally have. In Auschwitz, my only focus was the nourishment through the whole day, the soup, will it be thick or thin? My allocation of bread in the evening, will it be a decent slice of bread or just a small, not very thick enough, and that's about it."

I tried to indicate that I was comprehending this situation. "Plus, you couldn't control it anyway. So why worry about it?"

"Yes. I coped with it. I had to turn deep into my soul and get all the strength from there. So now, as I struggled to recover, I had to remember how it felt to be loved, to be cared for, and not just say that now I don't have it. What I had to tell myself was that I once was loved, I once was cared for. I had value. I had a family who did care for me. But that's all the value I had. Everything around me in the world I was surrounded with, it didn't matter to anyone. It didn't matter to anyone if I lived or died. If I am hungry or cold or if I'm hurting. It wasn't any person's job to keep me alive. I had to keep myself alive. I don't know if this makes sense to you . . . you cannot get strength or anything from anyone. You only have yourself. If you didn't matter to yourself, then you just stopped fighting for life and you died. It doesn't make sense to anyone in the world."

Helen began to take short breaths. I sensed the effort was becoming too much. "Because everyone, even today . . . I have a little dog and I matter to her. I didn't have . . ." she took a long breath in, ". . . after all . . . you don't matter to lice. And this is what is so hard to explain. That's why feeling that I am totally a one and only living person, I don't even know if *human being*, but whatever I feel, I am here alone and everything around me I am just imagining."

We both sat there in silence, staring mindlessly at Pup while she incessantly licked her paw, now red and raw from her obsessive habit.

"Pup! Stop licking!" Helen admonished her doggie. Then she offered me some lemon drop candies and picked up her thought. "After a total of two years following liberation, I was released. To what, I had no idea. Where does one go? Home? After so much suffering, the most important thing is a welcoming person to come home to. I felt the whole world was a merry-go-round and I fell off the horse, and the merry-go-round goes on and on, but I am not on it. You know, Valerie, I once spoke about this to a group of six hundred students at Arizona State University, and a young man in the audience later asked me, 'Were you ever able to crawl back on the merry-go-round?' and I looked at him and said, 'Not really, because once you fall off, you are just not the same.' Then I said to him, 'I bet you are a Vietnam veteran.' And he said, 'Yes. How did you know?' 'Because of the question you asked me,' I said. Then I asked him, 'Were you able?' He didn't answer. You see, I can understand how the Vietnam vets felt. After so much suffering, the most important thing was a welcoming person to come home to.

"Anyway, I always tell people that I never went home. There are some things you would rather lie about than explain. But that is not quite the truth. I most wanted to go home to my hometown because I knew we gave away a lot of things to my neighbor and I hoped to get some things back that belonged to me. It was no problem; my hometown was now occupied by the Russians, so it was easy for me to get permission. I went to my neighbor's home who now had my family's valuables, what were left. She let me stay for just one night. This was a judge's wife. And you know, she never gave me any of my family's things. She said, 'There are two reasons why I need it more: because you are ill and you might die. And if you don't die, they will take you to America and they will give you everything. I need it more!' Can you imagine? Can you imagine!

"Our house was next door. Yet, I never looked at it. After staying just one night there, I then took the train to the border. When I got to the border, it was a Saturday and it was pouring rain. There was a group of Jewish survivors who were staying there before leaving for Israel. They told me, 'You cannot pass out of here; they will never let you out of here. You were born here and they will never let you out.' You see, they had passports. I was born there, but all at once I was a Russian citizen. I was now in a land occupied by Russians. I said, 'Well, I want to try it, anyway.' Imagine that from a seventeen year-old girl! I could move around easily because I had no baggage. I had nothing in this world. So I hid in the train station, waiting for the next train that would begin to move. People were boarding one in which the front part was for passengers, and on the back end were Russian tanks under tarps to keep them dry in the rain. I knew this was my opportunity to get across the border, so I picked myself up and jumped onto the train and hid under one of the tarps when the train started to move. Passengers on the train, who had somehow watched this whole thing happen, applauded me the whole way. I was now in Czechoslovakia."

"And now you were truly free."

"Yes. Free. And alone."

A couple of days after seeing Helen, Tom and I were shopping in Scottsdale. Due to a local parade, we were rerouted through back streets that left us quite literally back in my old neighborhood, the streets of my childhood. "Hey," I suggested, "let's take the Val tour, Tom."

> *"This Urgent Care Clinic used to be Giovanna's house. And over there used to be a 7-11 we used to walk to in bare feet in the summer and buy Corn Nuts and Fizzies. Did you drink Fizzies?*
>
> *"Sure, remember the jingle?*
>
> *"Yep—'Hey, it's a happy Fizzies party!' Down this street I can see Giovanna and me going door-to-door selling Girl Scout cookies. Here's our little cul-de-sac. And the house I lived in from first grade till halfway through high school. This was my bedroom window. Alan lived next door, a mentally disabled kid. My dad caught his older brother looking in my sister's and my bedroom window right there! We had two mulberry trees in this front yard. My mom used to plant zinnias and petunias. And there's the Dursts' house—I think they even still live there. I used to babysit for them. And the Doyles' and the Vosses' where I fell out of their chinaberry tree. There was a ditch behind that house (the house wasn't even there then) where we had grand childhood adventures. It all looks so different now. It is all so different now. And down that street is the Blampedes' old house. They used to erect a huge Christmas display and broadcast blaring organ Christmas music whether you wanted to hear it or not. Of course, everyone did, I think."*

After we got home, I kept thinking about Helen. Why, I wasn't sure. Tom asked me what I was learning about myself through all this so far. I said I didn't know. I didn't know. Yet, something told me that my stroll down Memory Lane that day was a clue.

Rebuilding

I GOT TO HELEN'S HOME one day and she shared with me many struggles she'd been having all week. They might have been the usual annoyances of life, but for Helen, these challenges could bring on physical pain and even depression. I looked closer at her for a moment. She always dressed very warm, even on this balmy spring morning. After having learned about her skin's ultra-sensitivity following her lice infestation, I now understood why she was wearing a thin turtleneck shirt turned inside out to avoid the seams, then a light sweatshirt with soft lavender sweatpants and slippers. Her hair, a very light brown with tender graying roots, was neatly combed. She always wore a moonstone ring on her left ring finger. For being over eighty years old, she looked remarkably young. Her skin was very soft and her eyes a gentle brown.

I began our session with a question that I hoped would lighten her spirit, but with Helen one could never be sure.

"Helen, how did you meet your husband?"

"Back home he lived only eighty-ninety miles from where I was, and yet I probably would have never met him. But as it turns out, we were on the same refugee boat to North America. We were bound for Canada because America wouldn't take me due to my tuberculosis. I had a cousin I'd never met who was also a survivor and lived in Montreal with her husband. So my destination was Montreal. Jack's plan was to go to Canada because the Korean War was on and his three brothers, who were already in the United States, told him he should not come to the U.S. because he was twenty-one years old then and the draft was in place. There was a good chance he would go straight back into a war out of duty to fight for his country, even if it has just become so. Because his brothers had friends in Toronto, and it was close to his brothers in New York, that was his destination.

"We both took the boat at Bremen/Halifax. These refugee boats were different from other boats. Believe me, these were no pleasure crafts. It actually reminded me of the concentration camps because we were jammed in a boat that should probably take about 500-600 people, but there were about 1200-1300 people. Women and men were separated except at mealtime. And believe me, our food was, well, *bleh.* That's the first time I met with cold cereal for breakfast . . . terrible. I couldn't believe that was an American breakfast; it didn't taste good at all. At home, I was used to Cream of Wheat, or rice with milk. It was over this first yechhy meal that I noticed Jack Handler for the first time. There was my future husband, over six feet tall, incredibly well-dressed, wearing a French beret, and he started to talk to me."

She stopped, nearly mid-sentence and said, "Did I ever show you a photo of him?" Glancing around her small living area and noticing that none was on display, I answered *no*, even though she had shared one with me weeks earlier, because by then I knew that just talking about certain things was good for my friend. She needed to revisit wherever her mind took her. Helen went to her bedroom, where I now realized all her really personal items stayed close to her, and came back out with their framed 8 x 10 wedding portrait, faded over time.

"Jack Handler," she murmured, handing me the photo.

"What a striking, handsome young man," I commented, then she reached for it back.

She held it as if a valuable artifact and gazed at it. "He just seemed very different to me; he looked like a perfect gentleman. He even had a camera to take pictures of other people. Yet we had much in common. We both had Hungarian backgrounds. Of course we were both Jewish. Many of the people there were Czechs who were running away from the Russians who had now occupied Hungary and Czechoslovakia." She smiled at me and said, "If there is one thing Jews know how to do, it's immigrate. Why not? They've done it for thousands of years. The first was Abraham!"

Then Helen laughed and said, "But the truth is, the reason I made a connection with him is because he had Dramamine. I was so seasick, cold cereal and all. He offered me Dramamine, and that was it! There were other men who were just as tall and handsome that I was more attracted to, but he had the Dramamine. That can be more important than flowers or anything when you need it. I didn't even need food; I just needed the Dramamine." She laughed again in a light-hearted way I'd not heard before.

Wedding portrait of Helen and Jack Handler.

"We arrived in Halifax. The first thing he did was to buy an English newspaper, even though he didn't speak English, just so he could put my cousin's address on the top of the paper. Then, we separated—I thought forever. I didn't know why he even asked me for my address. This was in spring. Then, for the High Holy Days, which are in late September/early October, I got a Jewish New Year's card and he wrote that he works as a dental technician. He didn't ask me to answer, but it had his address. He told me later that he couldn't imagine why, without being able to read that newspaper, he never threw it away, that he took it all the way to Toronto." At this, Helen stopped and looked away, smiling to herself.

"I had obtained a visa to come to Detroit to find my uncle and aunt on my father's side. Detroit is very close to Toronto, so I thought I might as well stop in Toronto and just be with Jack for a few days. Well, I did and I don't know if it was love or loneliness, but he still looked very good and had a good job in a lab and he had a nice place to live. He waited for me at the station, which made me feel very good. He rented a room for me (I didn't expect him to) and even paid for it for a week and we decided we are going to get married."

"In one week you decided this?"

"Well, you know what's funny, we had corresponded for a whole year. We wrote back and forth, and that's the best way to get to know somebody. Before I saw him again, I had sent him this picture taken in Montreal." With this, Helen stood up, went into her bedroom and after several minutes, reemerged with a lovely, formal headshot portrait of herself.

"You were quite the looker, Helen," I winked at her.

"Well, of course I looked different on the boat and throwing up in the ocean," she laughed. "He loved my letters to begin with, and I'm telling you, I always was a pretty good letter-writer. The truth is, I needed security. It wasn't fun in Montreal. It was very hard. While I was in Switzerland, I had had training in hotel management, and even earned certification in it. So I had big dreams that I would make a career at this. But opportunities like those were not available to me. I didn't even have distant family to turn to; as it turned out, I didn't live with my cousin. I hoped she would welcome me with open arms, but she wasn't very happy to see me. She had a little place with linoleum on the floor. She and her husband worked at home sewing pieces for a swimsuit garment factory, and she had two children and she had a big bedroom and a kitchen; that's all she had. They were very nice people, but they really had very little. She kept her house so clean. Every Friday she waxed it, she cleaned it, she cooked, she worked hard. It was really very hard, and he had a heart condition. By the time

Helen's formal portrait taken in Montreal.

he was thirty-seven, he had a heart attack. By that time she had two children to support; she didn't need a refugee depending on her. Again, I felt homeless and alone. I spoke French, but a different French than

Canadians speak. I have to tell you, my life there in Canada, it was not very nice. I had just come from a sanatorium and worked very hard. I lived on very little support.

"I settled for a while in Montreal, but I couldn't stand the heat and humidity because I came from Switzerland. Too hot in the summer, in the winter, too cold. Montreal has terrible summers and terrible winters. So I was pleased when there was a job offered to me in the Laurentian Mountains for the summer by a woman who had a delicatessen store and rented out rooms. It was a very busy store with resort guests. They had Jewish and non-Jewish resort places in this community. The woman who owned the store had polio as a baby and was now a cripple. She dragged one leg in an iron brace. She and her husband were quite a pair in contrast. She was much older than he. Her parents owned a flower shop on the main street in Montreal and they were very wealthy, so they basically bought her a husband. He was a Polish Jew who came with the first transport after the war. He was tall, good-looking, quite younger than she was. He spoke very broken English; she was born in Montreal and spoke French. She had a baby with him, who was beautiful, perfect. I worked for maybe twenty dollars a week with room and board. She made me work seven days a week, twelve hours a day! She was jealous of me because her husband was nice to me. He just talked to me. Sometimes he bought me a hot dog. We spoke the same language."

By now Helen was lost in memories. "I dated a little, but I wasn't very happy. It was shocking to me because all the men I dated wanted to sleep with me. And I came from a background where one kiss meant you were going steady. I was now twenty-one years old. By this time I was quite the world traveler, having been through Poland, Hungary, Czechoslovakia, Switzerland, France. But all of my time was spent in their hospitals!" she snapped.

"So there were many layers to your decision to marry Jack."

"Yes, many layers, indeed. We married in 1950 in Toronto, but I didn't know anyone in Toronto. My wedding day came and the only person I knew was my future husband, not a soul else. He had a lot of friends, and his oldest brother and his wife came to the wedding. Now, we Jews have a superstition: the bride is not supposed to be alone on her wedding day. But I had no one. That morning, I walked from where I lived in a rented room to have my hair done. Jack knew that I was alone. I don't know what story he told his brother, but he sent him to the place where I had my hair done. Just because he knew I was alone. This was the type of thing—he was a perfect gentleman."

I decided to dig a little. "Helen, can you tell me a little about how your camp experience affected you in marriage with this relationship of love and intimacy, and also what it was like to be married to a survivor? Did Jack have his own issues and problems? Was that a factor in your relationship?"

"I wanted to get married because I was very lonely. He was exactly the type of person that my mother would have picked for me. He was very good-looking, with old-fashioned politeness respect, and wonderful manners. He had fine clothes. And he had a thirst for intellectuality that was incredible, especially since he came from a family who lived the religious, not in the secular world. He was very secure psychologically, emotionally, in who he was. Now and then we approached an incredible restaurant where we could not afford to have dinner. He would walk up to the maitre d' and ask him what the menu was for this evening, and they would tell him from A to Z and thank him for asking. He just exuded that confidence."

I said, "He's like my husband, Tom; he feels he belongs anywhere. Not in an arrogant way, but just in a sense of instant belonging. My husband didn't marry until he was forty-five, and had always lived alone. And I would ask him, 'Don't you get lonely in this house?' He always answered, 'Well, I kind of feel like the whole world is my home and this is just my room,' which I thought was a nice way to go through life."

"Yes, that's a lovely way to go through life. Jack's approach to other people was a little more like *how lucky you are to know Jack Handler*. Everyone loved Jack. We would go to a party, and he would notice every girl who had a new hairstyle." At this, she slowed her speech, hesitant to go on. "He didn't cheat on me, he just . . ."

I tried to help. "The whole world was his family?"

"I suppose so. That's because he came from a home like that. On my wedding day I was told the Handlers were the Rothschilds in the whole district."

"Did he come from money?"

"Money. And respect. But I would have never been able to marry him back in Hungary because of our social differences."

"So what was his Holocaust experience?"

"Jack would have never made it alone. He was spoiled and served by many grown-ups who had watched his every breath. He came from a very, very wealthy family. His parents were much older. He came from a generation where marriages were arranged. So good families went to good families. Even in the camps he was lucky because he had a brother who was just like him, a go-getter, who was twelve years older. They were together in Auschwitz. But he was in several other camps, working camps because he knew how to make deals."

"Did you see any way that Jack's concentration camp's experience affected him? Did it create problems of attachment?"

"He never talked about it and he was the only survivor in his family. He didn't even apply for the money offered to survivors. That was the Handler pride. 'It's blood money; I don't want it.'"

"How long was he in the camps?"

"Same as I was."

"Yet, it wasn't something the two of you talked about or processed together?"

"Never. No one talked about the camps or about family we'd lost; we all pretended that it never happened. That was a way we survived surviving. Jack didn't have any health problems. Psychological problems, I don't know. Don't forget, this was forty years ago. Psychologically, he wasn't as . . . he wasn't violent. Our son says we quarreled a lot, but we did very well together. As a matter of fact, we immigrated to Detroit about a year and a half after we were married, and we rented a furnished room, and from both our salaries, after a year in Detroit we bought half a duplex. We had two bedrooms upstairs and a living room and kitchen downstairs. We had a little backyard. We didn't have a garage, we didn't need one; we didn't have a car. We had friends, and we were very good to other people, to other survivors, who had children. Every time they needed money because they were saving to buy houses in the suburbs, we always lent them money without interest and they always paid us back. We trusted them, and they always paid us back. But eventually we bought our own little house in the suburbs. Jack was a dental technician for a while. Then he started a liquor store and pharmacy to make more money. I got pregnant and stopped working for awhile because I had lost a pregnancy before and wanted to be more safe this time. By that time we lived in Oak Park, a suburb of Detroit, and we had enough money for a down payment.

I was beginning to envision a whole other time period, another age, another culture emerging post World War II.

Helen went on. "After a while, I worked as a decorator at Hudson's department store. I liked that work. What was incredible was that when I filled out the application—that was a time when they still asked you for your religion. I was told ahead of time that I would never get a job at Hudson's because they did not employ Jews. But I was small, I was well-dressed, I looked like a little French girl. And they thought that I would be very good at the position, and I was, because when my customers used to ask for me, they didn't remember my name, they'd just remembered *that little French girl*." She laughed.

"At that time life was still so formal that I had to wear a suit and it had to be black, navy blue, or gray. No other colors. And I had to wear stockings. Jack and I went on vacation one summer, and I got poison ivy on my legs and it was all broken out and I went up to my supervisor and said, 'I cannot wear stockings because it will stick to me.' She said, 'Well your legs are brown enough (it was in the summer). For a month you may be without stockings.' But I had to have special permission for it. Can you imagine? And they never called me *Helen*, it was *Miss Handler*, not *Mrs*. But everyone was called by her last name, even between colleagues; they didn't even know my first name. I worked there for quite awhile—about five years —until I got pregnant with my only child, Barry."

"Yes, I want to talk about Barry, and what having him did for you. I know you were married ten years before having him. Had you been trying to have a child?"

"Well, we tried. The first two years we were careful not to get pregnant. It turned out I couldn't get pregnant that easily. When I think of all the fun I could have had if I'd known I couldn't conceive easily." She winked at me. "We spent a lot of money trying to get pregnant. I went to a specialist. It just didn't happen. Things weren't as advanced back then. Jack didn't have too many live sperm, but it could have been me. So we went for shots. Finally Jack said, 'I am tired of sleeping with you when the doctor tells me to sleep with you, when the thermometer says to sleep with you.' And so we said O.K., let's stop it. We went on a weekend cruise to Toledo."

I laughed, "Gee, that sounds exciting."

"And I got pregnant!"

"Well, they say that's when it happens, when you stop trying."

"But I lost it."

"Oh, Helen, that must have been very difficult."

"My doctor told me if I ever got pregnant again, then they would have to watch me very closely. I had to go every week for an examination. I had what's called an incompetent cervix, so there was a greater risk of miscarriage. When the baby reached twenty weeks, my body would likely expel it. It was a horrible time for me because it was an up and down time. For two weeks I hoped I am pregnant; for two weeks I knew I am not. Then for two other weeks, I hope I am pregnant, and for two weeks I am not. Finally the doctor told me, 'I am giving you pills so you will have quiet. Your nerves will relax because you'll know you cannot get pregnant. Take it for two months. You are a nervous wreck; you can never get pregnant this way. This is the time you should get pregnant because your body is full of hormones.' I said, 'O.K.' and went home. I never got my period. I got pregnant with Barry. But I practically lost him, too. I had to see my doctor and have a pelvic examination every week because of this incompetent cervix.

"But for the joy he gave me on the day of his birth, I will never be sorry to have gone through all that, nor all that followed. Barry was a beautiful child. I used to take him for walks. I was a stay-at-home mother the first five years. Every time I put him to bed I always said that if only for the pleasure he gave me the last twelve hours, I will never complain about him. He was so bright and good-looking. *I can't believe this is my son*, I thought. For me, the greatest joy is to have a child. I should breathe for him. When my son was born, I felt I had my answer, a reason as to why I was chosen to survive. I had a purpose. He was born and my life became valuable. God was generous once more. So I lived for Barry."

Helen paused, then slowly uttered, "And yet, if I wouldn't have had Barry, I would have never divorced Jack. Seeing me as a mother changed how he saw me as a woman. That is the truth of it. And . . . well . . . I couldn't live with him anymore." She stopped speaking and took in a long, slow breath. I let the silence in the room form its cocoon of privacy for her. *Tell me what you will*, Helen, I thought to myself. *Do not tell me what you cannot.*

"Was I *in* love with Jack Handler? No, not at first, but I loved him a lot. He had a lot to manage with me in our early years. I was afraid of others, especially of men. They could kill me like the SS I knew. I found myself afraid that Jack might hurt me like so many others had done. After all, I had seen the depths of cruelty in my life. But he was the type who totally took care of me. He never broke a dish in anger or hurt me. He was always there. I used to wake up in the middle of the night and just touch him that I wasn't alone in the world anymore. Jack always took care of me. He was just very good to me, and I really learned to love him. Even after we got divorced and I went through several surgeries, I never opened my eyes that he wasn't at my bedside."

Helen, who had been holding the framed wedding photograph all this time, set their portrait on the table, and said with an air of nonchalance, "So, this was my love story."

But I knew her true love story belonged to Georges, her lover from France, and I hoped we'd talk more about him in days to come.

Helen sent me home that day with a package of English muffins, an editorial from the *Jewish News* written by her rabbi, and Charles Colson's novel on presidential intrigue, *Gideon's Torch*, that offers the dedication:

> *To the heroes of Eastern Europe, known and unknown: the believers of every confession who defended the Truth, overcame evil with good, and toppled the greatest tyranny*

of the twentieth century. May their lives both inspire and caution us in the tumultuous times in which we live.

The menorah in Helen's kitchen window.

Self-made Woman

"VALERIE, I WANT you to do something for me."

"Of course, Helen. What is it?"

"I want you to go to Auschwitz."

Except that.

Helen and I had been meeting every week for several months by now. Each visit left me emotionally spent on my ride home, and sometimes for days to come. If I were to chart out our discussions, they would most likely resemble synapses of the brain for their viral, fragmented activity. Some days I recorded very little. Some days we needed to simply process her week, or current events. Some days she was so restless, I questioned whether this process was even healthy for her. On this day, she seemed particularly somber. Her statement caught me off guard.

"Oh. Uh . . ."

"Look," she said in a commanding voice, "I will pay all your expenses. You should go with my teacher friend, David, and his student group that he takes every spring. It is a nine-day trip. He's very good. It will be meaningful for you."

"Oh, I'm sure it would be. But I teach in the spring." By now I was an adjunct instructor at a nearby community college, teaching education courses to future teachers.

"Well, maybe he will schedule it for your Spring Break."

All of my deeply-rooted, severe aversion to the Holocaust bubbled up to the surface. I suddenly felt sick to my stomach. *Please, please don't be asking me this. Anything but this!*

"Helen, I just don't know. I'll have to think about it."

"Of course. But I really think you should go because then you will truly understand me."

"I'll see," I continued to stumble. "I'll see." I found it difficult to focus on the rest of our visit.

Luckily, my recorder did not have that problem.

"I want you to understand how I made it after I was now divorced and alone, something I thought I'd never be again. It seemed I was always trying to survive in life, but now I had a son to also keep alive with only $15 a week for child support. I did so many different jobs that you have no idea. Barry was starting to go to school and I needed a job, but I wanted to be home earlier when he came home from school. So I learned how to manicure, because I could do that and the hours were much better. I went back to Hudson's where they knew me and knew my good work record. So there I was in their salon upstairs. We wore pink uniforms, mine with my same name badge saying, *Miss Handler*. So when Barry went to kindergarten, he said to his teacher, 'My mother is Miss Handler.' 'No, you mean, Mrs. Handler.' 'No, *Miss* Handler.'" Helen rolled her eyes and chuckled at the obvious conclusion the teacher must have reached.

Then she paused, took a sip of her hot tea, and said, "But you know, I have had a hard time getting Barry to be proud of me. There was a time when I manicured in a men's barbershop. Barry wasn't very comfortable with it." Her voice lowered. "Someone from his school saw me there and told him that and he was . . . he was pretty upset. He was a young kid, like eight or nine years old." Then, just as quickly, she smiled and said, "I was popular as a manicurist, perhaps because I always had nice hands myself. When I was in the Carpathian Mountains, a young man and I had a crush on each other. And when I was leaving, because I was going on to France, I asked him what he liked most about me. People usually would tell me it was my eyes, but he said it was my hands. So I am looking at my hands and people used to say I had beautiful hands. One year Barry bought me a ring for these hands. Nowadays, my hands hurt. I drop things. They are swollen."

I leaned over to her and held her hands in mine, struck by how soft they were. And thin.

As if reading my thoughts, she said, "My bones are practically disappearing. I have no meat there. You touch it; it's just bones." I felt her wrist. "It's just bones, you see?"

"Is it because you've lost weight?"

"No." She points to her belly and laughs. "It's all here. The muscle deteriorates. And yet, I've always walked a lot. I used to lift weights, but I gave it up when my bones started to go. I couldn't do it because it started to hurt. I always had bone trouble because of the surgery for my tuberculosis. It did something to my spine. Yet, I used to buy shoes for $2.98 at a dime store and they never bothered me. Anyway, I worked as a manicurist for a long time. Later, I went back to school and did some accounting, but I wasn't really good at it. I did so many different jobs that you have no idea.

"Eventually I moved to Detroit, but I could not find a good job. It seemed everywhere I went I was not qualified. By the time I had earned enough education to apply for a job with the City of Detroit I was told that I cannot get one because these jobs were reserved for minorities. Here I was a woman, a single parent, a refugee, but I must have been the wrong minority; I felt like I had the wrong color, the wrong religion. So what could I do? I had no credit. Even Sears would not give me a credit card. I did not qualify, not because I had debts, but because I didn't have debts. It's crazy. So I found a way to create my own credit! I moved to Phoenix and started my own drapery store in Metro Center. I owned it for thirteen years. And because I didn't have credit, I earned it the hard way; I even *made* my own draperies at first. I worked seven days a week through the year and was able to give jobs to three people and put my son through college and law school with nothing borrowed from the government."

"You are a self-made woman, Helen."

"Yes . . . yes. I'll tell you a big secret: I didn't even go to the Jewish Freeloan. I did it totally alone. I remember when I turned for help to the Small Business Administration, I entered the office and there sat a young man behind that desk and behind him were all the framed diplomas and he told me, 'You would be surprised, Mrs. Handler, how many people come to me, and instead of having clear ledgers, bring their receipts in a brown bag.' And he looked at me and I had a brown bag in my hand that contained, yes, my receipts, so I told him, 'Oh, this is just my lunch.'" Helen sat up in her chair, lifted back her shoulders and giggled, clearly amused and impressed by her own resourcefulness. "So I built up my business without going to the banks, without getting help from the SBA, and just from living from day to day. Eventually, I could have opened other stores, but I only had so much strength."

We talked about what having a business meant to her, its demands and rewards.

"Do you know, Valerie, one of my employees was a young German woman who openly admitted that her parents were followers of Hitler."

"That's an extraordinary dynamic."

"She became a very good friend of mine."

"What was her name?"

"Elka. She came to the United States when she was seven, so she was very much an American. I hired her because she was a very warm, nice person and, you know, she grew up in this country. I had another sales girl whose name was Regina—like my mother—and she was an immigrant, well-educated, bright. She worked out very well. It's amazing, but it didn't bother me that she was from such a privileged background. I don't know why. Back then I was more open to human beings." Helen stopped here, lost in thought. "I am much more . . . I think the fact of what I went through all my life made me . . . I don't know, I can't find the right expression. I am not as generous emotionally as I was."

"You were softer then?"

"Yes. I find it interesting that people think that as people get older they get nicer, but it can be the other way around."

This was one of those moments in my conversations with Helen, when she would become very emotional, speaking either in a deeply sad tone, or in an elevated pitch of distress. She did not cry. Helen is not a crier, that is, in front of others. But I found myself trying to manipulate the discussion to reel her back in to a calmer state.

"What have been your sources, or have you been able to find sources for joy in your life?"

"Very little and usually a for very short time. I belong to a generation in which I never had . . . I was never . . . I never had the opportunity to be young, and now I don't have the opportunity to be old because of the way the world is. I think that I am in the wrong place in the wrong time. I was . . . I turned ten and eleven when young girls admired actresses like in the 1940s and I hoped I would be a teenager and wear my hair in a pageboy and play tennis and ah, go to dances and sit in cafes outside and watch the world go by like the young girls did then. But by the time I was old enough to enjoy it, I was wearing a yellow star. By the time I was old enough to live it, I was in Birkenau, and after the war, for five years I went from country to country from hospital to hospital, and when I got married, my greatest joy was to reach out in the bed next to me and know I belonged to another human being. Finally to have a child brought me joy. And even today when I look at him and I know how bright he is and how good-looking he is, I can't believe that this is my son. And to this day, he comes home every evening, tired from being in court all day, and he calls his mother and we talk.

"But we had our tough years. Every morning I chauffeured him to school, then did all my household chores and errands, then worked twelve hours at the store. And I didn't have a weekend free. I kept my house clean. I cooked for him. I took him to everything he had to go to. When he was in high school I drove him to the ice-skating rink and sat while he skated until 9:00 at night. I couldn't tell him I was tired. But I had dealt with people all day and had to be very polite, and my exhaustion sometimes left me with a temper, and he and I had many fights.

"I remember at Toastmasters, I gave a speech I titled, *When You Have Lemons, Make Lemonade*, and I said that right from the beginning that the greatest joy is to have children, but the greatest joy comes with great suffering. How come babies are born and they cry? Women are going through a lot of pain by giving birth and from then on every growth includes also pain." Helen reached over to the candy dish on her coffee table and scolded, "Valerie, trail mix, you didn't have any!"

"Oh, I will, really."

We talked on and on about the challenges of being a parent, particularly a single one. I could tell Helen was carrying the mental and emotional burden of raising a child by herself, something I related to having been a single parent myself for several years. Finally, I asked her, "Did you ever want to marry again?"

She hesitated, seeming to be struggling internally about whether or not to say what she was thinking . . . or remembering.

"It wasn't easy. Yes, yes, I really wanted to. But it wasn't easy. I didn't want to marry just anyone. Do you know, I never dated an American boy. I was a very cute divorced young woman. Jews, especially, just wouldn't date me; I had an accent like their grandparents and they didn't want to go back there. They didn't want to go back to anything European. They wanted to be American. Everything they knew in religion and science was European, but they didn't remember that. They knew Einstein was European, but that was Einstein and I wasn't. It was very hard on me. You know why? Because I will never need anyone as much as I needed someone then. But I was always first a mother."

I began to see a profile form of a woman who would forever be greatly challenged in her life, but one who also grabbed each circumstance by the shoulder and said, "Come on, show me whatcha got!" The resilience of the six-year-old played itself out as she propelled herself into the role of single parent and independent businesswoman.

"Did you enjoy your work in the drapery business, Helen?"

"I was never a decorator. But I catered to my audience. I knew what would sell. What the customer wanted. My customers were mostly blue-collar, but they had good money because Phoenix was growing on the west side. I respected their taste and gave them what they wanted. I used to tell my customers, 'Good taste is how it tastes to you. Who says someone has better taste? For your money you are entitled to your taste!' I made them feel they know how to do it. After all, they have to live with it after the decorator leaves. And if they don't like it, it will never become their home. I taught that to my employees."

She must have noticed my slight glance around her living room, unconsciously sizing up her own taste. "The pictures that you see here in my home? I didn't hang them; my friends did when they redecorated my home for me. They surprised me while I was recovering from surgery. And what they didn't redo stayed the same. I've never done a thing to this place. It comes from never having felt I had a *home*. Why, I made my living in decorating, with my drapery business. But I feel all this does not belong to me. I could walk away from it. I make no attachments." Helen paused for several moments and finally said, "Because I know it could all be taken away in a moment."

She rose from her chair and suddenly announced, "You must be warm in here! I'll turn on the air conditioner." When she returned to sit down, it was as if she pulled herself back to happier times at her store.

"One day during lunch, two of my employees were in the back together and I stayed in the store. A lady came in and said she wanted a 'really nice bedspread.' They were stacked from the shelf bottom to the top of the wall. Now, I am not comfortable on a ladder. I opened one bedspread and another and another and with each she said, 'That one does not make me happy.' I finally said, 'Madam, if it's the bedspread that will make you happy in the bedroom, you have a problem already!'"

"I'll bet she walked out."

"Oh yes, she walked out."

We both broke into easy laughter.

Helen continued. "I enjoyed the business for a few years. But the one thing that used to upset me was when a customer ordered custom-made drapes from little samples of custom fabric. 'You know it will never be 100% same color.' I always made that clear. Then one would come in and it was a half shade off or it was cloudy or sunnier that day. It would seem like their whole life was ruined because a drape was a little bit off. Then I'd remember all the pain and hunger in the world and I'd think to myself, how can people be so concentrated on their own desires? I can't live with it! *Argh,*" she snarled. "I had customers from Sun City who I knew would never buy, just old ladies who liked to shop. But I was patient and spent time with them. One in particular I must have spent an hour with. Eventually she said, 'I'd like to buy it, but I don't live here.' 'Where do you live?' 'Sun City.' Well, Sun City is only ten miles away!'" More laughter.

"One of my employees, Alan French, was very loyal. If I had to leave work quickly, or had an emergency, I could call Alan. He would take me to the hospital, then tend to the store. More than an employee, he was my friend. I taught him so much about life. He always sat at my desk and took in everything I said. He was so patient. And good-looking. All the ladies in the mall loved him. One girl came in during her lunch hour. 'You know her,' he said to me, 'she works next door.' 'No,' I answered, 'she works the whole mall.' We laughed and laughed at this one. I could tell it was a story she'd told often and one she'd never tire of.

"My dear friend, you have a wonderful sense of humor," I told her.

"Yes, I know I do."

"You tell great Jewish jokes, too."

"Well, maybe telling jokes I enjoy for that moment."

Yes, this was a good day at Helen's. They weren't always. There were times when I sat across from Helen and wanted to bundle her tiny frame into my arms and hold her to my chest to comfort her. There were moments when I would look into her deep brown eyes and want to collapse in my own tears. There were mornings I wanted to run out of her condo screaming, shaking fists toward heaven. And every single day with her I wanted to right her wrongs, and the world's.

But on this day we laughed like old friends.

I called my friend on her birthday to wish her a happy one, only to find out that no one had made any plans to be with her. That can't be, I told myself. So I drove out to her place and took her to her favorite restaurant for lunch. After a full meal, she was leaving the restaurant and stopped to take a couple of their bread samples.

"I like bread," she said, in an attempt to rationalize more bread on a full stomach.

"No, Helen," I offered, "you collect bread." She smiled and nodded.

Before I left her that afternoon, I told her that although she had next to no visual remnants of her childhood or family, I wanted to get to know her better as a young woman through any photos she did have. She seemed surprised, yet pleased, that anyone would be that interested, and agreed to share what she had with me. That next Tuesday I walked into her living room to see a worn and weathered photo album, a baby's scrapbook, and a small shoebox sitting on the coffee table. For the next two hours, she sat alongside me on the sofa as she and I shuffled through hundreds of old photos. Jack Handler as a young man, Jack and Helen as newlyweds next to a new car, Helen in a business suit, the two of them on holiday, young parents pushing their toddler in a swing. More than once, she stopped and walked into her bedroom, coming back out with large framed formal portraits: her wedding day, another glamorous head shot of her, Barry as a baby, Barry as a toddler, Barry in high school. I gently held each photo in my hands, taking long moments to look deep into the faces of Helen, Jack, and Barry. Theirs didn't look any different than any others found in vintage shots from eras long ago—dog-eared edges, faded sepia or muted colors. But what the photos could not say aloud rang loudly in my head. I knew what no one else looking at these could ever know. Why, I now knew more about them than I knew about some of my own relatives. And the stories I knew were painful to reconcile with their images smiling back at me.

I picked up one photo that I couldn't put down. A tiny, black-and-white image showed a beautiful young lady wearing a dark, turtle-necked sweater, and lying propped up in a hospital bed. She had long, thick hair that cascaded in curls down her back, a slight, engaging smile on her face. Next to her bed was a large window that opened to the lovely evergreen landscape of what was her sanatorium home for over a year. The back read *1947*.

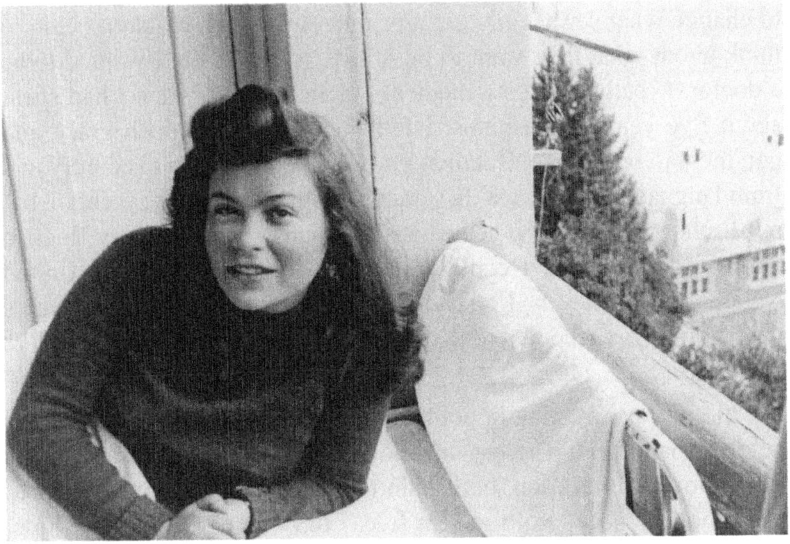

"Helen, this is you?"

"Yes."

"You are beautiful!"

"Yes, well, I had my good years," she grinned.

I was transfixed. I could not take my eyes off of it. Far from the unavoidable signs of aging now earned by my octogenarian friend, this woman looked young and vibrant. I looked close at her lovely countenance and was mesmerized by one whose beauty transcended the years she had already survived. She looked like someone I might have known in school. She looked like someone I would have liked to have known. For a moment I felt like I did know the young Helen.

"May I keep this one?" I politely asked.

"Oh, I suppose so. Yes. I am glad you like it."

"Oh, I do. It's beautiful. I will cherish it. It makes me wish I knew you then."

She looked wistfully at me as if she did, too.

We carefully restored her photos to their resting place as I said, "Helen, I'm wondering, what career would you have chosen for yourself if your circumstances had been different?"

"I would have liked to have been a doctor. My little universe began to change when I was only eight or nine, just when children begin to think about what they want to be in life. At that time, I wanted to be a doctor. I really wanted a medical practice. Later, when I had spent about five years in hospitals, I felt that it took so much grace and goodness to be a nurse. But then I moved from country to country and from language to language. In Canada I could have gone to school, but my French was French, not what Canadians speak, and my English wasn't good enough. I could have been a translator for the United Nations where they had a school in Geneva. I still have the papers that show I was accepted to that school. I could read and write in five languages.

"I didn't like anything in politics. I ended up attending a school for hotel management. The organization that supported me was willing to pay for my education, but I didn't have any money for living. But at the hotel school I got food for free. I have a degree from the hotel school. When I got to the United States, I should have gone further, but I didn't want to pursue that. I also was a woman and this was 1948-50. Remember, I couldn't get a regular credit card from Sears. By the way, there is something I would like you to have."

I was getting used to gifts from Helen. But this one I did not see coming.

She went into her bedroom and was gone for what seemed like long minutes. I sat patiently, stroking Pup who sat next to me on the sofa. Finally, Helen came out carrying something small in her hand.

"This is one of my most beloved possessions. I want you to have it."

What she placed in my hand was no bigger than my hand itself. A tiny gold-ribbed box, which held its own tiny maroon grosgrain-covered book. Resembling a missal, complete with satin pages and gilded edges, it looked like a treasure lost in antiquity, its title etched in gold—*Great Love Poems of Dante Gabriel Rossetti.* My breathing stopped.

"Oh, Helen. It's beautiful."

"Yes. It is from Georges to me. Look inside."

I read the inscription: *To dear sweet Helen – One of God's gentlewomen. Freeport, August 1972. "Go forth and put thy hand into the hand of God – that shall be to you better than light and safer than a known way."*

Each crisp page contained a selection of the stunning works of Rossetti's poetry.

"The timing was never right for us to marry. Too many complications of family and religion. But he was my love. He was very special to me." Always back to Georges.

I felt I was being handed two souls.

"Helen, the significance of you giving this to me goes deeper than you know. I adore the works of Rossetti and all of the Pre-Raphaelite Brotherhood. It is my favorite literary movement in British literature that I taught for so many years. Most people are completely unfamiliar with them, so it is doubly meaningful to me that you share this with me. I will cherish this on many levels. Thank you so, so much."

That day I drove home tormented by the words, "what if . . ." *What if Helen had been born in a different time and place? What if she had been a man in the same era? What if she hadn't been born a Jew? What if she hadn't lost her whole family? What if she had married another? What if she had had greater opportunities, benefactors, gifts of grace? What if I had never met her? What if the world could have known those millions of others? What if . . .*

Religion...Justice...Love

WHAT DO YOU GET when you mix a secular Jew with a wayward Catholic? We were two women who questioned everything, searched the universe for answers, and valued the art of rich conversation. Our visits always left me drained, yet exhilarated, by the intellect of my friend and our heady discussions, which more often than not took us through labyrinth-like journeys into religion, philosophy, and politics. Each week we delved deeper and deeper into our individual beliefs and the conflicts that emerged from them. Helen considers herself neither a Conservative nor Orthodox Jew, yet there is no mistaking her commitment to her Judaism, nor the impact of her heritage.

It seemed like each week we met, something that had happened days before had left Helen upset. Sometimes it was something that could not wait for Tuesday. She called me one weekend, more troubled than I had ever heard her.

"Valerie, I must share this with you. I am so angry!"

"What's wrong, Helen?"

"The *Jewish News* just published an editorial that speaks to the subject of forgiveness. Well, I cannot forgive. I cannot! The editor states that we have the power to forgive. The power, maybe, but do we always have the r-r-right?" Helen was now nearly shouting into the phone. "The editor writes, 'I think an apology also needs to follow with a question: Will you forgive me?' I must respond. I must say what I think about this. So I have written a letter to the editor. Will you listen to it?"

"Of course."

"Here it is:

> *"As I speak to thousands of students and others for the last twenty-five years, I am asked this question over and*

> *over and over. "Can you forgive?" It is a question I have struggled with in the depths of my soul for more than sixty years. I live now in a free country and was able to rebuild my life. I do have the power to forgive for my own suffering. But I belong to a group of people for whom six million is not just a number; it means my family, including my nine-year-old brother and my seventeen-year-old brother. I knew their joys, I knew their tears, I knew their plans and hopes for a bright future that they never had a chance to fulfill. Do I also have the power to forgive for those unfulfilled lives? The question isn't "Do I forgive?" For me, to forgive is not a free choice. The question really is, do I have the right to forgive?"*

I heard the pain in her voice, feeling it virtually rush like a current through the phone lines and I could almost see her pounding her fist on her chair cushion.

"I have to tell them what I think. I have to. Who are any of us to forgive on behalf of another?"

She spoke on in anger for about forty-five minutes and seemed to find a morsel of respite in the act of sending off her thoughts, which were published in the following edition.

When I came to her home the following week, she was still upset about it.

"On the 50th anniversary of the Nuremberg trials, Senator John McCain was a guest at our Days of Remembrance, what, in Hebrew, as you know, is called Yom HaShoah. I was president of the Phoenix Holocaust Survivors Association. And we had close to a thousand people who came—several judges, most of them Jewish. We had many lawyers, also mostly Jewish, and we had Senator John McCain as an honored guest. When I opened my speech I said, 'As far as the judgment at Nuremburg is concerned, I always somehow hesitate just even saying this title because who am I to have an opinion when we have a U.S. senator here with us, several rabbis, several judges, several lawyers? Isn't it pretentious of me to express that opinion about Nuremburg? But I am a Jew. I am a Holocaust survivor. I am a woman. So who will prevent me from expressing a judgment? Who was the prosecutor, who was the defendant, who had the right to judge those crimes? Who was on trial? The Nazis? Were they on trial? The Germans? Was the whole world? Was God? How can you bring a judgment for six million murders? The Torah says *Justice*. And *justice* shall you pursue. It doesn't say, *Bring a judgment*. It says, *Pursue* it. Somehow deep down, I always felt that the Holocaust was a shame on all humanity. Did the world learn? No. The world learned how little value human life has. Where is the hope? If there is hope, it will take more than a couple of generations. I just hope that in the future the world learns that judgment isn't enough. You have to make it never a necessity to happen.' And when I stepped off the podium, I asked my rabbi, 'Did I have a right to include God?' He said, 'Yes, you did have the right to ask God if He feels He has the right to judge.'"

She went on. "It's amazing that somehow the world, most of the world, learned about the Second World War, but killing never stopped; it just increases. I always feel the tragedy of the Holocaust. Our slogan is *Never Again*, but hate in the world never stopped, killing never stopped, so somehow we must come to teach our young children who didn't live it, who only heard about it, that they cannot commit the same mistakes that generations after the first World War kept on committing over and over. But the Nazis dared to show humanity that killing is acceptable, that life is very cheap. Where is the fact that Life is the greatest gift that God gave humanity?

"When I visit classrooms, I always tell the children about Genesis. Is Genesis God-inspired or just inspired by human need? To me, it doesn't even matter. Whatever it is, if we came up with the story ourselves, it's the best story we human beings ever came up with because it clearly says, *God created a human form out of dust,* but then *He shared His breath with that form* and now that first human couple, and for the rest of human existence, we carry a little of God deep inside us. We all share in that breath, and so we are all connected. It never says in Genesis that Adam and Eve were white, black, red, or yellow. They were human beings. It never said that Adam and Eve were Jewish, Christian, Muslim, Hindu, or any other religion. God only expected them to be as godly as they can manage to be. This is the goal and the obligation of every human being—that we should grow. We are not born perfect, but we are not born sinners either because God does not create sinners. If we are all God's children, then we cannot be born sinners because we are His creation. And we have come to a point, maybe not being perfect, but advancing goodness, just an inch further than our fathers did, and inches more than our grandfathers did."

"How has that formed your life's philosophy day to day?"

"We have in our holy books a sentence that I feel very close to. When a Jew raises his cup for a drink with his friends or family, we do not drink to success, to health, to happiness, to friendship, we only have one toast: *L'Chaim*. To Life. It doesn't say what life. My rabbi friend in Orlando, Rabbi Sherwin, always said, 'Life is not bad. Life is not good. Life is.' If God gave you life, from then on it's your obligation and becomes your goal to make it grow in you. When you wish someone well, you say, 'May you grow from strength to strength.' And you should use that strength to improve the world. It is also taught in my religion that you don't have to finish the job, but you must start it or move it along a little bit."

"I like that."

"You see, most of us aren't moving it along. And I hate to say that the sad part is that the leaders are not. I just hope the teachers are. And this is the tragedy, that there are many countries where the teachers teach hate. Adam and Eve did not have a religion. God wants to be honored by all human beings in a way that it makes *them* feel the most righteous. So whoever you are, if you are good—what God calls good—then you are in the right religion. Every religion that I know of teaches you to help your fellow human being and respect this beautiful world that God created for you. I have a little saying that my rabbi sent me. It says that God tells you, 'If you honor me, I love you. If you hate me, I will be passionate with you. But if you see or cause your fellow human beings to suffer and don't help him or her, then I am sorry I ever created you.'

"You have to fight for life every day; you cannot fight for life tomorrow. *Today* is the day when you have to fight for life," Helen slapped her hand on her lap. "A baby knows that, the minute the baby is born. And when the baby gets hungry, he doesn't wait, he screams right there. And when a baby hurts, he screams right there. So we were created with the right tools, but somehow as we go along, we get too scared, too comfortable, procrastinating, and we lose it. But the truth is, today is the day! It's all we have."

I nodded. "I've always seen the primary obligation as humans as following the model of the three-legged stool. We are here to serve God, our fellow man, and ourselves, in a way that serves all. If you think about it, if all our actions are in honor to all three, we just cannot go wrong."

"But you must prioritize these. My order would be Self, God, and our fellow man. In my religion, you come first; you can do nothing unless you're O.K. God gave you your life; you are responsible for your life first. There isn't such a thing as Judeo-Christian because our religion was made for you and then for everything else. We are a religion of deed, then of faith. You are a religion of faith and out of faith comes the deed. But we are a religion of deed. If you do well, you don't have to go to church. I don't say we are right, I say this is the way it is. You see, we are not a religion of love; we are a religion of justice. Justice comes before Love. You are supposed to be decent, even to people you don't love, because you cannot love everyone."

"I disagree," I answered. "I think we can love all. It is a matter of how you define and exhibit love. If I believe that we are truly connected, as one living, organic entity, then I have no choice but to love every other human being as a part of my own existence. I used to teach John Donne's *Meditation XVII* in which he wrote what's become the cliché, 'No man is an island unto itself.' His point was that all humankind is a member of the same metaphorical body. Well, what if it is not so metaphorical? You know, the advent of thermo-dynamics has made scientists rethink so-called independent organisms. An enormous aspen grove in Colorado, previously, thought to be comprised of hundreds of separate trees, was discovered to actually be one huge single structure. It's the Gaia principle, that the planet is one living, breathing, completely interdependent organism. So, what if we are literally connected by a divine energy, thread, spirit, whatever term you like? How would that affect our actions, were we to prove this? *And therefore, never send to know for whom the bell tolls; it tolls for me.* Am I affected by the death of another, even one whom I do not know? Yes. The human body, if you will, is the less for it. Now, certainly, ego gets in the way, but that is when we must return our thinking to a Gaia-like principle and recognize that another's fortune or misfortune does affect me. That is where the direction of my deeds lies."

Helen sat forward in her chair, her voice becoming agitated. "You learn from everyone, even the things you shouldn't do. You have to feel to do the deed. If you do a deed and you do it for a reason, maybe it advances you. It's much more pragmatic; it's not all just beautiful. You do many deeds that will do you good, too, but as long as it's good for the people. Our forefathers, including God, weren't perfect, but we accept it. Moses wasn't perfect; Abraham wasn't perfect; Isaac wasn't perfect. We talk about their mistakes every week. We discuss it. We don't accept it; we discuss it. There is a story in the Talmud that tells us one rabbi said, 'Let's do it this way' and the other three said, 'No, this is right, no this is right,' and then the sky opens and God says, 'No, the rabbi who is alone is the one who is right,' and the three said to God, 'You stay there. You created the world and now it's up to us. And if we make the mistake we pay for the consequences!'"

We laughed.

"Judaism is a religion of justice. Even if you act on love, love is sometimes destructive. So you can't just use the word *love*. To say that everything has to be connected to Love is false reasoning. No, you cannot love the people in another continent; you can't even love everyone in America. The word *love* was used in the New Testament constantly as the point that leads to everything, but that's not true. The New Testament says, *Do to your neighbor what you want your neighbor to do to you.* Not emotionally, just intellectually. You see, the New Testament was translated from Latin, not from Hebrew. And that's where the mistakes are. The Ten Commandments do not say, *You shall not kill*; it says, *You shall not murder*. Now, there is a difference. You may kill in self-defense, but never anyone in the back. But if you are in danger from the front, you can kill. But once they turn and you kill in the back, then you are guilty. It is murder, done out of rage. But think how many times that is misquoted and misused."

"Man is very skillful at doing that!"

"Yes," she nodded. "When I was involved in the Great Books club, one of the chapters was in King James and the first line said that Jesus was the descendent of King David 'through his father.' I was the only Jew in the room and I said, 'I thought he doesn't have a father!' So you tell me how. It is the first line. Well, it just does not make sense to me. I had heard it all my life. I wasn't a stranger to Catholicism; I almost married a Catholic. And I went to many churches in Europe and in the sanatorium they always took us to midnight Mass. And there were certain things I loved about it. But Judaism is what I am made of. Judaism is very hard, but it's who I am."

And as a gesture that my day's lesson in Judaism had come to completion, Helen sat back in her chair and began stroking Pup who lay oblivious in her lap.

My friend and I spent many hours like this. Many days, with only minutes left in our morning's visit, she would suddenly say, "But enough about me. How is your family?" scolding herself aloud that she hadn't asked. I often sensed that a part of Helen truly wanted to "get together with the gals" and merely "dish the dirt," but hers was just so much deeper and heavier. Yet, as our months together stretched out, I clearly felt a lasting bond of friendship building between us. Helen let me know in many ways how deeply she cared about me. I knew from all she shared with me that I held a unique position of intimacy with her. And yet, intimacy—or rather attachment—was something she always struggled with.

I once asked her, "Do you feel that for the rest of your life you've not been able to connect emotionally to people?"

"Yes, particularly since my son grew up, and he was no longer a child whom I could hug any time I want. I still even feel it with my dog. When I watch her, I *melt* from love, but when she approaches me, it's not the same. I miss seeing my son every day terribly. I love him. I miss him. It's practically a physical pain how I miss him. And yet he walks into the room, I can't even go over and hug him unless he hugs me. I have the desire, but yes, I'm totally closed."

"I suspect it's that when we can't control our emotions, we therefore control our thoughts to keep those emotions at bay."

Helen nodded. "Oh, yes. I feel that I would like to scream it out to the world, but I don't know how to make that connection. I am a deep philosopher, but I'm a stranger even to myself. And that's why people

. . . people want to help me, but they really don't know how because I am on that hill totally alone and everything else around me is only my imagination. Nothing exists. It was killed. And I have lived for more than eighty years. I can cry for the whole world; I am hurting for the whole world. And I don't know if I always was such a complicated person or just became so complicated, but I know I am. I live in a paradox: I am totally closed in, but if I am closed in, why do I have such a strong desire for closeness?"

"Maybe because that's the human element."

"Yes, it's the same thing. I get homesick and I sob, but it's my pain. It's very hard to explain. The desire is more painful. It can never be fulfilled, because I don't know how to fulfill it. I am most alone. Saturdays are the hardest for me because there is no one to call. I don't know anyone so totally alone. I cry like a child." She paused. "I miss my mother the most."

Helen stopped and gripped the arm of her chair. I sat quiet, allowing her to travel where her thoughts took her. Finally, she continued. "When I was in Auschwitz, I never believed that my mother was dead. I knew it, but I didn't let it be. Of course I knew my father was dead, so I prayed to him to help me to survive. So I believed in it when I needed it. But through all that horror, I clung to a dream. I had to live. I must survive to tell my mother about it. I knew she will be waiting for me, take me in her arms, love me again. I will cry and tell her what I had been through. She will kiss me, protect me, reassure me that from now on everything will be all right, that I am safe once more, loved and protected once more. She will reassure me that it was only a bad dream, that the world is O.K., my life is O.K. and I am home." Helen took in a long breath. "She was forty-two when she died. If she were alive . . ." Helen suddenly became quiet.

I looked at her, and behind the tired face of an octogenarian, I saw a child's pain that knows no age, no expiration.

Her eyes gazed down at the floor, and I wondered where else her mind was taking her. Finally, she said, "I don't know . . . I have seen five psychiatrists and why is it that no one ever went as deep as you do? Basically, you do more for me than any psychiatrist because they all treat me out of a book, the way they learned how I am *supposed* to be.

But they don't hear me. And that's why they can't help me. Or maybe there is no help. Period. But you, you, Valerie, are asking questions that no one else has. Maybe because you listen to me longer."

"Is that all right?"

"Yes!"

"I am glad to hear that. There are so many, many important ideas and feelings you've shared."

"And it's a lot of work for you. I know that I am a very complicated person. It's not like telling the story of the Holocaust only. It's a story of growing up, it's a story of a family, of a human being."

"It's about a life."

"Yes." Pup looked up at her as if suggesting *I'm part of this, too.* "Do you see this little dog? Well, for a while after Barry left her with me, if I went close to her, she went with the teeth like a threat. I was scared of her. Don't forget, we had German shepherds in the camp; every Nazi had a German shepherd. That's why I never had a dog in my life. I only felt sorry for her; that's why I took her from Barry. She was Barry's dog for two years. When his career got so busy, he didn't have time to take care of her and insisted I take her. At first, she was scared of me and I was scared of her—of this little dog! I finally called my veterinarian and I asked what I should do, and he said, 'You do not get scared. You remember that you are the boss. You make sure that you let her know this. Don't hit her, but say *no* very strongly and don't give her food till she comes to you asking for it.' I never did that. But eventually, she changed; she got used to me and I got used to her. But I was scared of this little dog! I'm still scared of Barry when he screams. He doesn't scream at me. But he's used to speaking loud because he does trials. And because that's effective."

"Was your husband like that?"

"Jack was a good man and a good husband, and he would never hurt me. He would never lay a finger on me to hurt me. And yet, some nights I would wake up and feel petrified of him. I would have to come out to the living room and sleep in a chair. I was terrified he would hurt me. And yet, he never would."

"Was it just his being male, and larger than you?"

"Yes, it was what he *could* be, oppressive authority and strength over me, that just would panic me at times. You know, a few years ago I had a terrifying experience. I had a panic attack. I needed to call someone, but in my state of mind I had forgotten everyone's phone number, including Barry's. I only remembered my cousin Kathy's phone number and I called her up at 10:00 at night and I said, 'I have to come over to you. I am afraid to be alone in the house.' I closed the house, held my keys tight in my hand; I was having a full-blown panic attack. I was sitting on the stairs outside in my robe and nightgown when she came and picked me up. She came all the way from Scottsdale. She took me to her house and as she was pulling in she said, 'There was something funny; you were not answering what I asked you on the phone.' She took me to a hospital. For twenty-four hours I didn't know what they did to me. They took my brain scan, all kinds of tests. Everything was normal, except me. I did not remember the twenty-four hours that totally disappeared from my life. I didn't even remember that Kathy had come and picked me up. When I woke up I was in the hospital, but I don't remember any of the five tests they took. Through all this I still had the store to run."

"So once again you went to another place in your mind to disconnect."

"Yes. That's why since then I never drive home alone after speaking, when I am my weakest. It takes too much out of me. I am at my weakest, and I am afraid the panic will come back. If you want me to speak, you have to pick me up or I'll get a ride from my friends. Anyway, I think I told you enough about myself for one day."

Tikkun Olam

I SHOWED UP THE NEXT WEEK with banana bread for Helen and treats for Pup. Helen had had a difficult week. Physically, she was struggling with her heart medication, all-over body pain, and sleeplessness. Emotionally, her depression was exacerbated by world events that left her low. And Judaism could be applied to all. My religion lessons continued.

"I must tell you, Valerie, I doubt God so many times; I really struggle with it. Yet I pray to Him every day. I keep giving Him another chance because He's supposed to do the same for me. God has a covenant with us: when we sin we are supposed to learn from the mistakes we make. If it happens next time, we are not supposed to fail and sin again. So it's not an ongoing thing that you can do it over and over. In order to be the human being God wants you to be, you have to repent your soul for the people you have sinned against. Yom Kippur is the time to learn from your mistake and turn to God. But first you must ask for forgiveness from those you've sinned against. If you are not forgiven, you have to ask a second time and ask a third. If the person you seek forgiveness from is a good Jew, he is obliged to forgive you. But you are not truly forgiven unless you do not repeat it. First you have to apologize to the person you hurt, pay for the damage you did. And then you can ask God to forgive you with the condition that when it happens all over again, you will not commit the same mistake. Also, when we pray to God to forgive us, we talk about all the sins of *all* human beings, including non-Jews, all sins made that year. 'We killed, we stole, we were cruel . . .' It doesn't say 'I was' because whatever happens in the human world, we are partly responsible for it. There is a word in Jewish tradition: *Tikkun olam—improve the world*."

"*Tikkun olam*," I tested my pronunciation. "This is a wonderful concept," I said. "We need more of that, to be sure."

Pup jumped up on to the sofa and into my lap.

"Pup! Improve the world, get off!" she laughed, Pup panting. "You see, God doesn't have to improve the world. He created a good world. It's up to us. The mistakes that we make are made by humans, and we're supposed to improve our situation. Now, I am not telling you this that you should convert; I am explaining to you what we are. We all have heard about extreme situations in books and movies when people are forced to resort to cannibalism. No one ate anyone in the camps. They starved, but they did not touch the bodies because that would have made them pagans. And to turn away from God and being pagan was one of the reasons one deserved to die. That's a deadly sin. There are three things that are deadly sins in Judaism. One is to turn to idols. One is to commit incest. One is not to believe in one God.

"We talk about the Ten Commandments. We note that it says, *Honor thy mother and father*. Notice it does not say, *love*. There is no *must* to love your parents, but there is a *must* to take care of them, to honor them. And we talk about that all the time. Sometimes when you steal, you actually take away someone's life because maybe what you took was absolutely essential for them to live. Also, when you help someone you should never take away his dignity. In the Jewish tradition, we use the analogy of each member of a community farming one section of a field. God gave you the field and the wheat on it that it grew, but it doesn't belong to you alone; it belongs to the people who need it. Sharing of your harvest with those in need is expected. You are not supposed to humiliate the people who need it. It's not a perfect religion, but it taught a lot of lessons of humanity that didn't exist before because even the Greek and the Roman philosophers or now the Hindu philosophers tell you how to improve *yourself*. Meditating doesn't help other people. Closing yourself into a cloister does not help the world. It makes you a saint? God doesn't need more saints. I can see that the person who loved all animals has a day of his own in your church."

"St. Francis."

"Yes. Because he helped living things. But just saving your soul is not enough. You can save your soul by helping the hungry to save their souls. You know, I was thinking the other day that the Constitution says all human beings are created equal. First of all, that's not quite true. As long as all human beings are created good, they don't have to be equal; each has his gift. Good people see the need right away and want to help. Do you know that in the tabernacle when they were going for forty years and they carried the tabernacle with them—everyone was to give a half a shekel? The same for the poor and the rich. The rich were not supposed to give more, the poor were not supposed to give less. That made everyone equal. That doesn't exist anymore.

"Anyway, I am the last one who says that the Jews always follow that because there was no Jewish civilian in the detention camp in Germany after the war. There were some Jewish soldiers who were the liberators, but we had, believe it or not, Swedish students who in their summertime came to help the sick ones. There were no Jewish nurses who came to help."

"Why was that?"

"Because they are human. We were the untouchables. But when I came to the western United States, these people were so friendly, they talked to each other, they smiled at you, they asked you to their homes for dinner. I am telling you, when I came here, the people were incredible. Is everyone great? No, but we are not all so bad, either. We are on equal levels."

"Most people here today are still from somewhere else," I added.

"Yes, and they come here making friends. Maybe because they started from scratch in this country; they all needed each other. Friends are available here. You meet them at the grocery stores, in the pharmacies, at the gas stations, in the classrooms, at Costco. Everyone smiles at you. And it's not that way everywhere, believe me." Helen, suddenly smiled at me, and said, "I am glad I am doing this book with a non-Jew, because what I'm saying is interesting to you."

"Helen, do you believe, either within Judaism or not, in a heaven and/or hell?"

"I never made up my mind. For eleven months after someone dies, Jews say Kaddish because we put in a good word for someone. They are not here, nor there. I read an article from an Orthodox Jew who said that and he said that Hell is like a rehabilitation house. You go there to clean your soul and after you clean your soul you go over to heaven. Do I believe in it? I don't believe in it one way or another. I have a hard time believing when no one ever came back and proved one way or another." She smiled.

By now I felt close enough to Helen to ask, "Did you ever feel God's presence or the presence of anything spiritual when you were in the camps?"

"I wanted to talk with you just about this very thing, so it's amazing you asked me that. The people who survived, I don't know, I can't speak for others, but I lived for the hour. I became a different person in the camp because by my nature I analyze, I believe, I am a philosopher, I read. But I was totally, totally different there. I concentrated only on 'I can take it.' This is not so bad. I actually was starving, but I told myself, 'I did it. I went through the whole day; I can take it.' I wouldn't have survived otherwise. I became a different personality because right after the liberation, once I was more or less free I became right away who I was before and who I am now."

I didn't know if Helen realized she was moving our conversation away from my question, but I wanted to know more about this metamorphosis. "So you did return to yourself, but a changed self?"

"Well, not to my old self. I jumped from being a child to being old. I never was a teenager. I became a grownup."

"I know you lost that developmental stage. I wonder, did you ever go through a period much later where you made up for what you were denied, say, when you were thirty years old, and start acting like a teenager?"

"No, I had my responsibilities. I was thirty-three years old when my son was born. But I became my adult me. Whichever country I was in, I saw the people clearly, but I never went back home, not only physically, but mentally or emotionally either. When I tell you that I cry like a fifteen-year-old child, I'm not like an eighty-year-old who cries like a fifteen-year-old, but I *am* a fifteen-year-old. I jump from one period to the other. When I find myself back in camp, I am a teenager, but not a teenager like here; I am the person who existed then. I actually feel as cold and as hungry and as everything else as I felt then. People say that each part of one's life is another chapter. Each part of my life is another book, not just another chapter."

"You said earlier that even God is not perfect. Explain how God is not perfect."

"I don't know if He is or isn't perfect. We don't make Him perfect. It always amazes me that Jesus is made out to be perfect. And he really wasn't."

I added, "I tend to agree, because that's the whole point, that He was human. If He was God in human form, then He's not in divine form and human is not perfect."

"I can't imagine God in a form. But we do it too because at the Seder we say, *and God reached out with His right hand and liberated us.* So we give Him a hand!"

The end of our morning's visit had come. I had a headache and was glad to step out into the sunshine back to the mundane comfort of everyday life. As I walked down Helen's steps, I looked back at her and Pup and waved, holding on to that day's gifts: a bag of candied cranberries, a book on reincarnation, and a lot to think about.

The next Monday morning Helen called to tell me she would be on that evening's local news. Now, that is not that unusual an event. The greater Phoenix community has long held Helen Handler in esteem and she is often their first contact for Holocaust issues.

"They are auctioning off Nazi memorabilia and wanted to talk to a survivor. Someone gave them my name."

"Well, I'll be sure to see it and we'll certainly talk about this first when I see you tomorrow."

A controversy had been brewing in Phoenix over an auction of Nazi memorabilia that was to take place later that month. The items included Nazi flags, SS soldiers' hats, and a plaque of Hitler. Perfectly legal. Perfectly creepy.

The next day I asked her, "Did you already know about this auction?"

"No, I found out yesterday. The Jewish Federation suddenly started to receive e-mails about it. People demanding, 'Do something!' So they found me. They called me and they were here in ten minutes."

"Tell me how you feel about it."

"It should upset everyone!" snapped Helen. "What they are doing is giving life to something that killed. They are feeding hate. I feel that it shouldn't be touched out of respect for our children. These collectors seem to be, some of them, very taken by the military aspect of it, which glorifies it. But ever since these children were born, or even the generation before them, we seem to be constantly in the middle of a war. And what shocks me is that we are not defending this country. In the Second World War, where Europe was attacked—France and England—America wasn't going to get involved. The people were screaming 'No!' It took Pearl Harbor for them to finally accept that America has to get involved because now America was attacked. But now I always felt that the war in Vietnam, in Korea, and now in Iraq, are all for political reasons. And I am very hurt about it. We actually sacrifice our children, and we are not changing anything in the Middle East. Arabs are still killing Arabs. Muslims are still killing Muslims. And we are not even talking about how many Christians are killed by Muslims. And of course there is Israel. When I turn to God, I always ask, 'Since the Second World War started, God, is there a quota how many young children have to die every year? And don't we fulfill and go over the quota?' Why are we doing it?"

Helen was sitting forward in her chair now, fingers tapping. "It reminded me that so many Torahs were burned, so many Jews were burned, and Hitler actually collected Torahs and all the sacred things we used for holidays and everyday life. He was going to have a museum in Prague that would show the world these used to be a people that we, no, *he*, destroyed, and they don't exist anymore. That the world only has now white, brilliant minds, like the Germans. And we are doing it with German artifacts."

I suddenly remembered that Helen has a heart condition. As her vehemence was growing, so was my concern.

"These symbols inspired the German people, they inspired the German soldiers, they dictated hate, they dictated horrors. What we are doing by displaying and selling them is, we feed the world with hate. We tell children that this has a value! Simply because people buy it and pay for it and people who get the money, use the money, that gives it value. So for money we can sell hate; for the money we can sell all the horrors that western civilization ever committed. It cannot change my past. I know these symbols. I don't want our kids to know them. I speak to children about obligations to the world. I speak to children to improve the world. I speak to the children about their responsibilities to *their* future. It shouldn't include symbols that represented death. I want symbols that represent life. I want symbols that display respect of one human being for another human being, and not those that dictate that we are not all God's children and that we are not all equal, we do not all equally have the right to this beautiful world that He created. Our children can see enough hate on television. Our children can see glorified death on television. I want them to see how life is glorified.

"I wasn't shocked by what the war represented. I know it. I dream it. It's imprinted with blood in my soul. But I want to protect the future generations from this. In a country where our children, our young people, are dying in other countries to establish democracy, in a country like that we should not have a value on symbols that represent fascism, that represent destroying children, and that's what hurts me. Not that I have to look at it. I never forgot them; I live with them!"

As if to snap us both back to the present, she abruptly stood up and announced, "I didn't make you coffee."

I offered to help, but she seemed to need a few moments alone. She slowly made her way into her kitchen and stood silently for some time before the coffee preparation began. *Is this where I hug her? Hold her? Try to cheer her way out of this subject?* I had to remind myself that despite looking the contrary, Helen is not fragile. And she definitely does not solicit pity. I let her dictate our dance. In Helen fashion, when she returned with our coffee, she picked up her thought right where she had left off, being not fragile of mind either!

"But you see, I even said that this is an insult to the second war's veterans. This is an insult to all the miles and miles of white crosses and Stars of David. It is betraying those graves, and strictly out of money." Helen set our coffee cups down and said, "There is something I would like to give you. It was given to me by a class I visited, but I don't need it, and it makes me think of you, so you should have it. Here." She reached over to her coffee table, picked up a small brown box and handed it to me. I opened it. Inside was a wood-carving of an angel with the tag, *Angel of Remembrance*. "You are keeping the memory going, Valerie. You and others like you. That is the ultimate *artifact!*"

I cannot think of a visit when my friend had not given me something to read, look at, keep, or borrow. And always, there were many things to think about. Newspaper articles about Holocaust books, movies, or speakers. Her own editorials. Letters from grateful teachers. A small mention from a paper about a documentary by a Catholic priest that set Helen off on a rant about popes and priests and the Crusades and Catholicism. And food. Always food. I prayed I was giving her enough in return.

The Voice Speaks

WHAT PROVOKES the voice to speak? What prompts the soul to shed its protective skin of silence and anonymity? What drives one to relive, over and over in a public setting, the pains of one's existence? Lying dormant within the diminutive frame of Helen Handler lay a powerful voice waiting for its time. Her time came long after her liberation. It came long after years of adulthood and parenting. But when it came, it began with a fairly innocuous drop of water and arrived in a tidal wave.

I asked Helen how she finally began to speak of her experience.

"I never talked about it until I joined Toastmasters, and only there. I only gave one speech about the Holocaust and it was not about myself, but about *Schindler's List*."

"Was it a matter of not being able to talk about it, not wanting to talk about it? Or did you just not have the right setting?"

"No one in my world talked about it. You must understand; no one wanted to hear about it. They talked about the six million who perished, but they never talked about us, the ones who walked in their midst."

I added, "I do know that when Wiesel was trying to get *Night* published, it took him ten years because no one wanted to publish it. Too depressing, they told him. Nobody wants to read this."

"Yes. When the world finally talked about the survivors, they talked about immigrants with the accents who came to New York, who worked in the sweatshops, not those in their very communities. I tried so hard to be like everyone. All I wanted was to be normal and blend in, participate in the life around me. Years went by, good ones and mediocre ones. I had a husband, a house, I matched carpeting, drapes, tried new recipes, gave parties; life was normal. But deep down inside of me there was that nagging pain, eating away my inside like a cancer.

"Is that what prompted you then to join Toastmasters? Did you come to a point where you wanted to talk about it, you needed to talk about it?"

"Noooo, that's not why I joined," she smiled, thinking back.

"Did you want to win friends and influence people?" I laughed.

"No. When I was single again, I dated a guy who told me one evening, 'This is the night I go to my Toastmasters meeting for singles, so how about you go with me?' Well, I didn't know anything about Toastmasters. But I knew a lot about being single. So I thought, why not? I had no idea. To me, Toastmasters was a toaster!" We both laughed.

"So this wasn't part of a plan? You never knew this was going to start you on this whole new journey?"

"No. No. Every guest has to introduce himself. I knew I would open my mouth and say my name and they would know that I am not an American—I have an accent. But then I thought, I deal with salespeople in my job. I really need using my English. Before, if I had to make a phone call in English, my heart was in my throat. A phone call! And I said to myself, you cannot run a business like this. And so, I did it. And it didn't seem to matter to anyone. So I joined. They met in the evening. It was a singles club. And he dropped out. After three or four months you give your ice-breaker. I was still worried about my thick Hungarian accent. I froze when everyone had to say his name and what he or she did that week. I remember saying that 'Most of you are Americans by birthright. I am an American by choice.' I ended it with, 'I had a customer who came into my store and said, 'If you don't give us a good price on these drapes, then we will send you back home!' I said to him, 'Sir, this is my home.' When I finished speaking, everyone applauded. Can you imagine? And that was the first time I won the week's prize." She pounded her chair in her usual emphasis, and smiled with pride. "After that, I went back every week. It just worked for me. I remained active in Toastmasters for seventeen years and winning twenty-three awards! The boyfriend didn't last, but I had found my calling. There used to be a Toastmistress club. When I joined Toastmasters, I was the first woman who was a finalist! I was the first person in my club who reached the finals. This little foreign girl. Can you imagine?"

Yes, I can imagine.

Helen's face was now lit up in enjoyment, remembering. "I always knew what to say and some of the things were really very funny. I had a speech where I said . . . about family recipes that everyone has a family recipe that no one has except everyone has. And you know, at Toastmasters you start with, 'Mr. Toastmaster, fellow toastmasters . . . My recipe is a *shit* list. Yes. My grandmother would always say, *You shit a little bit o' dis, and you shit a little bit o' dat. And finally comes out O.K.* You know why? Because *shit* means in Yiddish *to pour*. So you pour a little bit of this and you pour a little bit of that."

Helen speaking at the Toastmasters International Conference, Prescott, Arizona.

We both laughed and laughed. Sweet cream in a bitter brew.

"And you know it sounds all the more cute with your accent; part of your charm," I said.

"Yes, yes." On and on we laughed.

"Were you enjoying it?"

"Yes. I enjoyed it. I spoke about why you should raise your children one language, not bilingual, why you should give your children the present before you give them the past. You have to raise your children where you belong, not where you used to belong. How you must make them a home and this is your home. And tell them that God must have planned to have suffering and pain part of life, because it is our way that we are born, so there had to be a reason for it. And I explained to them how a shell gets a piece of sand and suffers and suffers before it becomes a pearl."

"So you always had philosophies and lessons of life. Do you still have those speeches?"

"I never used notes. I simply talked about life. As I gained confidence in speaking, I realized that my story needed to be shared. I found my voice."

"So, was it difficult to speak formally the first time?"

"No, I enjoyed doing it. It was as if I had done it for my whole life. I remember I opened with a joke. Being single, I gave them this one:

> *There was a wonderful movie showing and the movie house was crowded and before the movie started, a young lady on the end stood up and shouted, "Is there a doctor in the house?" and a man stood and said, "Yes, I am a doctor. How can I help you?" "Would you want to marry a nice Jewish girl?"*

I loved hearing them laugh, and I knew then that there will always be humor in my speech."

"Have you always had a sense of humor, Helen?"

"Yes, but no one ever believes it that I do, unless they really know me."

"Oh, I would believe it. I guess I really know you now. As a child, you probably could talk yourself out of trouble or maybe make someone laugh, like maybe your papa. Make him laugh, then you wouldn't be in trouble."

"Well, I don't know, but my grandfather used to say I was a real female; all I have to do is blink with my eyes and the tears start to come down. I was no big beauty, but when serious people gave me a serious compliment, they always said I was a very interesting person. So maybe . . . my son thinks that if I had been born in this country I would have gone to the top, but the fact that I had an accent, kept me from that. I guess that I am not as smart as Henry Kissinger," she said.

I needed only to look around Helen's living room to see evidence of her remarkable tenure with Toastmasters. Her walls and shelves display plaques and trophies spanning twenty years. This involvement, coupled with her leadership role in the Phoenix Holocaust Survivors Association, led her to broaden her public speaking to synagogues, churches, schools, and various community events. Anyone who is fortunate enough to hear her speak is forever altered. Whether to a small group of senior citizens, or a filled auditorium of six hundred university students, or a bulging, energetic class of forty junior high students, or a seminar for city officials, whether she has a microphone or a podium or not, Helen walks into a room and by her very presence commands attention and respect. Her spirit has a way of reaching across any space to grab the heart of each person in the room. Always preferring to stand, and with no notes, she encases her listeners with her tale and, more importantly, her message. In words of poetic poignancy, she somehow makes clear the horrors of the Holocaust without exploiting her experience for the sake of drama. Hers is a message of hope and love and improving the world.

And yet, there remains an audience of one who has not arrived.

"My son does not want to know anything about my experience. He has such a hard time coping with it because it is his mother. It breaks his heart. He doesn't ever ask about my family. Why, he doesn't even know my brother's name! One day, when Barry was in the first grade, he came in from school covered in mud from head to toe. 'What happened?' I screamed at him. 'I got in a fight,' he told me. 'With whom?' 'Karl.' 'But Karl is your best friend. What happened?' 'He said something about you.' 'What?' 'He said you talk funny.' 'Barry, you tell him that I have an accent. But,'" she paused, with a gleam in her eye, "'I have it in FIVE languages!' 'Yes,' Barry answered, 'but one of them is in English.' That shows you what a struggle he always, always had with his foreign-born mother. It is hard on children."

"Has Barry ever heard you speak?"

"Yes, when I got the Shofar award. You know that we light six candles at every commemoration and it's usually survivors who each light one. Barry was offered a candle and he accepted. It meant a lot to me that he participated. But when I looked at his face as he lit the candle, it was as if a mirror had shattered." Helen dropped her head, took in a deep breath, and continued. "No, he doesn't come to hear me speak. And really, I don't want him to. He's not the only one. We wanted for so long to form a second-generation group here for children of survivors, but we never succeeded. It always makes me sad to think about it, because there are more than enough of them. There are many, many, many of them. But this generation would rather put it out of their day-to-day life.

"All over the United States, second generation children would not like to deal with their beginnings. It's too painful to know what their parents went through; it's too horrendous. It's too painful to know why you don't have grandparents. It's too painful to know why your parents have heavy accents. You want to be like all other American children. It's too painful to know why your parents have weird behavior and speak 'funny.' One survivor said he used to think he was adopted; his parents behaved and spoke so differently than he. How did he turn up in this family?"

"Does this distress you?"

"I understand it. But it hurts. But they are all like that. It's very hard to walk away from parents if they live in the same city. If they live in a different city, you just don't get involved. The Jewish-American children want to be American, blend in. It's always been like this. Amazing that there is anti-Semitism in America when Jewish children try so hard to be American. They want to know all about their grandparents *before* the Holocaust—where they came from, what they did, what they were like. They want to know them, but not as survivors. A lot of this has to do with how their parents protected them."

"Is that a bad thing?"

"They knew what they went through. They still believe in the melting pot. Other nations believe in the salad. You know, there is a difference between immigrants and refugees. I know the difference, but even people in my situation are not . . . I shouldn't say bright enough . . . but many have street smarts. I have philosophy smarts. An immigrant comes to the U.S. because it is a new world and he or she wants to participate in this new world."

I nodded. "They are going *to*, versus going *away*."

"Right. An immigrant is fulfilling a dream; a refugee is trying to survive and rebuild a life. The refugees have no choice. Even here when they talk about the Mexicans, they don't realize that most of them are refugees. They would rather live in Mexico and speak Spanish."

"That's true," I said. "When I've talked about this issue with people and they say, well, there should be greater penalties and that would keep them from coming over. I say, no it wouldn't. If you are a father and your children have no food, no matter what you are threatened with, as a father, you will risk anything for a better livelihood. They are risking their lives to come over here."

"Oh, yes, you are right, Valerie. And we Jews should know; we are very successful immigrants because we have thousands of years of practice," she said with a wry smile. "We lost our homeland, starting with Abraham, so we learn to survive every place under any situation. Our children do not speak Yiddish, not a word. Do you know, my son doesn't speak Yiddish or Hungarian."

"Does that make you sad?"

"It never did, but it does now." Helen seemed to drift into unspoken memories of her beloved son, then her eyes softened again as she spoke of his successful law career.

I asked her, "Do you believe that, either spiritually or philosophically, things happen to us to prepare us for a later event, that some overriding providence prepares us, equips us for what we will need later?"

"Well yes, but it doesn't happen to everyone. Why isn't everyone so endowed? I think a person happens to have the genes."

"It's in one's fabric."

"Yes, or you don't have it."

"And isn't this the question that plagues so many of us all the time: Why were some people able to escape, survive, resist evils, and others not; and yet you yourself said you felt you had reached your end if liberation had not come when it did. We all have the point at which we cannot go any further."

"Well, my body couldn't have. In that barn, I was unconscious, I was without food, I was without water. So there is a limit to how far the body can go without food and water. I think your belief in God helps you, but it's your *belief* that helps you, it's not God who helps you. The belief helps you."

"What a startling distinction," I said. "Just the other day I was watching a debate on the merits of religion and one said, 'Well, all the evidence is there that people who go to church are healthier and more prosperous and they live longer, and her point was that it's because of one's relationship with God.' And I'm thinking, not necessarily. It might be the very act of that community and the praying and the taking care of the self inside and out that creates one's better fortune here, but that's not necessarily because God is smiling on you because you go to church and therefore you're going to be healthier."

Helen nodded, agreeing. "This is exactly what I am telling you. In the Torah it says that God told them, *Build a covenant and I will be there.* He doesn't say, *I will help you build it.* Do you understand the difference? God says you build one and then I will be there. It's your belief in God that helps you. Come on, when newborn babies went into the gas chamber, did He help them? Where was He? It's the people who survive whose faith in Him helped them. As Voltaire said, 'If we didn't have a God we would have to invent one.' Well you see, we believe in one god, but maybe because we realize that the people who believed in many gods, like the Romans and the Greeks, their culture was amazing, but their belief was wrong. It's not because many gods don't exist and one god exists, because yes He exists if we *believe* He exists. If we decide He doesn't exist, then for these people He doesn't exist."

"Is there a god for atheists?"

"I always believed there is a God for atheists because if not they wouldn't have to deny it."

"The paradox."

"We have no proof. You guys have proof because you have Jesus and you have all those saints." She smiled.

I was enjoying this conversation. "I sometimes wonder," I said, "with everyone's different concepts of heaven, hell, the afterlife, wouldn't it be interesting if whatever one thought it was, was. In other words, one is constructing what one's god is: Is he peaceful? Is he a war god? And your idea of an afterlife? Whatever you think is what you'll get."

"There is an article I want you to read. It is actually an editorial in this week's *Jewish News* by our rabbi." She got up and walked slowly to her dining table, shuffled through a stack of odds and ends of papers, finally finding the one. Sitting back down in her chair, she handed me the neatly cut out editorial and said, "Read this on your own at home, not on my time," and chuckled.

As I glanced through the article, I said, "I would have these types of discussions in class. When I'd teach Dante's *Inferno*, I'd choose a day when the students, and these were the best of the best, would come in and I would have just one question on the board: *What if there were no Hell?* And these were the kind of kids who, on a good day, I could ask one question and then just sit back while they would just zig-zag constantly discussing as I kept it going. Then we took it further to what if there were no Heaven? How would that change your behavior today toward your fellow man? Would it make you misbehave? We would have great discussions about this. I just think it would be interesting if people who believe in a god of peace, that's what they would have and those who believe in a judgmental, vengeful God then that's their construct, their reality. Alas, none of us knows the answer. It could be that everyone's right. For them!"

"True, we do not know. I always wonder about people like the Pope. After all, this is a very intelligent person. But when he speaks, does he really believe it or is it a political power? Does he believe that Mary was a virgin and God created a child in her? Many things in Catholicism, or in Christianity, worked politically for them. After all, they were Jews to begin with. But that doesn't mean . . . are you kidding, our rabbis did the same thing. We used to kneel. Christianity didn't start the practice; Jews knelt! So then we stopped kneeling, except for only once a year on Yom Kippur, but only very religious Jews go to the floor. Never through the year. But, yes, we did it first."

She folded her hands. "We used to pray with our hands this way, but once someone else prayed that way . . . you have to remember, we were so few that they had to change it. So that was a political thing, but it became a religious thing. It started out for politics and now, God forbid, it's a sin. Do you know what I mean?"

"I do. And if you take a look at the Christ story, different elements of the Christ story, particularly the Nativity, can be found hundreds and hundreds of years earlier in other cultures, identical elements of the story."

"The same with Judaism, what they came up with, they were not the first ones. The one god existed before, but he didn't succeed because the intelligent Romans and Greeks had many gods. When Judaism came up with one god, other religions took up with it. Would it have existed if they would be the only ones who stayed with it? If Christianity wouldn't have come, would Judaism have survived? The messiah is our concept, but our messiah never came because when he does, there will be peace in the whole world."

"And you believe that is still to come, do you not?"

"Yes. When we can prove it's here. Not everyone believes. We talk about it. About one percent believes that it will come. We don't believe that we will rebuild the temple. It is Christianity that believes that. There will be a second coming, but all Jews have to be in Israel. All Jews have no room in Israel unless you guys give us back everything around it that we used to have that we don't have, because the Arabs think that it belongs to them now. You see, religion is politics."

"Oh sure, always has been. And power."

"And power," she nodded. "It's all about power."

As I left that afternoon, Helen stopped at her door, took my hand, and said, "You know, Valerie, you know more about me than any psychologist because they never have the time. They listen to someone right after they listen to someone else, all day long. I know I am so complicated. Some people are complicated instinctively. I am brain-complicated."

"Yes, some are complicated externally by what happens to them, and some internally, but you are both. What a piece of art you are," I said, and she smiled.

"Well, what I am sharing with you is the person I am. So you see, when you said, 'Yes, I will write your story,' you didn't know what you were getting into."

"No, I didn't!" I laughed. "I didn't know *what* I was getting into, but I knew *that* I was getting into."

"Well, I owe you a lot because you listen to me."

Does Helen not know that I am the one who owes her?

To Israel

MANY DAYS as Helen and I sat in her small suburban living room, our discussions gradually wove their way into an exploration of God and the meaning of life. Other days, it began at the front door.

"Good morning, Valerie," she greeted me as I stepped across her threshold, "I am glad to see you today, because I have been thinking about something that I must share with you. I am reading a fascinating book by a theologian who makes many bold suggestions about God in our modern world. And I have a question for you: why do you think Man cannot agree on one view of God?"

Mind if I set my purse down before I answer?

"I ask this because I see this as both our curse and our blessing. It is the foundation of our diversity, which is essential for the species to progress, yet it leads to our greatest destruction."

"An interesting thought, Helen. There are lots of identities for God. People see God in many ways. Deists see Him as He created the world but He sat back and lets man run it. He is not involved in our day-to-day life."

My friend nodded, "That's the Jewish concept."

"Oh, is it? Football players thank God after a touchdown or pray that they win the game that day, and are convinced that God is interceding on our behalf, or not, at every moment in our lives. So what is your concept of God? Does He judge us at the end? Was God simply the creator and the rest is all up to us? Do we meet Him after this life?"

"You have to remember that I had to survive in Hell."

"That's why I ask," I said.

"I feel that when everything fails, if you believe in God, if He exists or not, that belief can save you; it saved me. I talked to God constantly when I was in camp; He was my life jacket. And I never, never doubted Him for a second, because I knew that if I let go of this life jacket, I would never be able to find it again. It was a faith that was so outside of my existence that I never had the courage to doubt it. If it would have disappeared and I would have had to justify what was happening to me and I couldn't have. So it was a leap of faith. It wasn't logic, because if I would have to explain—*How come that I was here?*—I couldn't because I hadn't done anything so horrible yet, then I could never go back to it. So no doubt whatsoever. But I remember talking to Rabbi Sherwin, my favorite, my only rabbi, on Yom Kippur. I said, 'I'm supposed to ask God to forgive me for the sins I committed this year. Well, why should He do it? I cannot forgive Him, because before you ask for forgiveness you have to forgive. And I probably can never forgive Him . . . yet.' And I wonder, can He forgive Himself? But I turn to God because I don't have any other place to turn."

I could see Helen's body tense and she seemed to be having an internal argument with her deity. "I used to walk up and down here and scream at Him, 'I believed in you when there was nothing to believe in. You took everyone away from me. You owe me peace in my old age.' I didn't pray. I spoke to Him with anger. 'If you do exist, do something!'" At this, Pup seemed to sense her rage, and popped up onto her lap to soothe her. "People ask me what liberation felt like. I never, never felt more free than after the liberation. I had no one and I had nothing. I had no change of clothes, so I didn't have to worry that I didn't look right. So what? It didn't matter. Maybe that's it. Having no one meant whatever happened only happened to me."

"And that's all any of us really has is the Self. It sounds corny, but it's in the song lyrics: *Freedom's just another word for nothin' left to lose.*"

"Yes, you see, that was it. The clothes on my back someone just gave to me. It might have been because I lost my first home at six years old. Moving into my grandparents' home didn't make it my home. When there was something that I wanted and I couldn't have, while before I could have had it automatically, now I was always told by my mother that, 'you are living on the generosity of your grandparents.' I was reminded many times that it's not my home. There is no word in English, if I want to translate word for word from Hungarian, it's 'bread of charity' with *bread* meaning all basic things. 'Remember, you live on the bread of charity.' And that's how I live even today. My mother used to say that we are here on the bread of compassion. I am not allowed to spend on myself. My mother taught me always to be grateful for what I have. And maybe when my mother used to say that, that's when she taught me to live for what I have. That has ruled my life. It taught me to survive. It taught me to endure. I never thought about it that way. Because on the other hand, it took away all my . . ." Helen seemed to be searching her brain, asking it to go from Hungarian to English, "my self-confidence. I am not a confident person; I just know how to play one. When I have five hundred children in front of me I know they are here because I am speaking!"

"You play it well."

"Yes, I do. Even as a child, after my father died, I felt I'm alone and everyone else, including my family, are people that I imagined, so maybe that's why I was afraid to leave on a vacation. I have told you that I get very homesick even today. When I have tried to go on vacation, I have had to come home the next day out of homesickness . . . as I am telling you, it starts to make sense to me . . . that when I come back, they won't be here and now when I cry, I am full of pain because it's true; I left and survived. The whole world that I had is not here. I don't have anything from my home. I don't have *anything* that belonged to me as a child or to my mother or to my family. Nothing. Even that picture of my father wasn't mine."

I felt my heart breaking to be in the company of an eighty-two-year-old orphan. A motherless child. A soul without a home. What could leave one more lonely? Suddenly I understood the impact of my recent tour through the streets of my own childhood. I recounted my experience to Helen. ". . . and steeped in this nostalgia I kept thinking of you and I didn't know why. I had to come home and write about it. I now realize I was feeling a kind of appreciation for my stable childhood and for the fact that I could so easily drive right through those streets again and point things out. My house is still there. I can still feel like it is my home. And I just kept thinking about you."

"Well, you think about it even when you are not with me, so it's part of your life now. You know, the closest I ever came to a sense of home, was the first time I visited Israel, and even then I was left feeling alone. I was a part of a group of a hundred people from Phoenix. I was the only survivor in the group."

"What was that like?"

"I was beside myself in anticipation; everyone in our group shared this. Throughout our flight, the excitement in the cabin of our El-Al plane was mounting. We could see the shores of Tel Aviv. 'We are home!' everyone shouted. Most of us had never seen Israel, yet all of us knew that this was home. For two thousand years, there was no state of Israel, but every Jew always knew that it always did, and always would belong to us. This Promised Land, given by God to us, and not the politicians!

"As I stood in Ben Gurion Airport, a thought crossed my mind: This is the first time in my life that I am in a place where I have *roots and rights*, as I called it. I was born in Central Europe, and was able to trace back my family there for five generations, yet I had no rights. I was a Jew. Now, I have been a citizen of the United States for fifty years, and I have rights . . . but not roots. But as a Jew in Israel, by the Law of Return, I have rights here, and my roots here are thousands of years old. The memories I gathered on my trip to Israel will stay with me forever. Three experiences impressed me the most: the military cemetery, the Holocaust Museum, and the Wall of Jerusalem.

"The military cemetery is long, with endless lines of graves, all exactly the same. High-ranking officers next to privates, no difference in their graves. The message is clear that each lost life was precious. The age of the soldiers clearly marked on the gravestones: 18, 20, 22, 19 . . . Everything inside me screamed, *Why, God? Why?* All these children never had a chance to live. Why? The answer came to me slowly. It was so simple. The Holocaust survivors have a motto: Never again. That is the answer. That is why these young people died. Jews may live all over the world, but here they have a home. Never again will a madman plan to destroy them while the world stands by silently. Never again will Jews go to the gas chamber because the doors of the world are closed to them. Never again. Because these young people died to protect them.

"Everyone who goes to Israel visits Yad Vashem, the Holocaust

Museum. For me, the children's exhibit was very powerful. I entered a pitch-dark corridor and was instructed to hold onto a rail and move slowly forward. As I stepped through the blackness, I heard names being recited. They were the names of children who had perished in the Holocaust. Two million children. Above me in the darkness floated tiny lights, each one representing a child. I watched them and wondered: which two belong to my brothers?

"In the museum's Valley of the Vanished Communities, I saw huge boulders reaching up to the sky. Each boulder was inscribed with the names of towns, whole communities of people that do not exist anymore. There were five thousand of them. I found the name of my own hometown and remembered . . .

"As a child I was lucky. I grew up surrounded by the love of two sets of grandparents. I remember watching my grandfather pray. Although I didn't understand Hebrew, I recognized one word again and again: *Jerusalem*. I asked my grandfather why. He explained that every Jew has a dream to set eyes on Jerusalem and that his or her bones will be buried in Jerusalem. Sixty years later, standing there in the Holocaust Museum among the names of dead cities, I realized I am the only one from my whole family who could live this dream. My family members have no bones. Their ashes are scattered around the fields of Auschwitz. So I stood there among those boulders, looked up to the sky, and called out their names, one by one. 'Welcome home,' I told them.

"Jerusalem. The Holy City. In no other place in the world do the past, present, and future blend together more than they do here. The cobblestones under my feet are more than three thousand years old. Can you imagine? Yet, on their foundation, the new buildings reach up to the sky toward a strong future. The noise that surrounds me talks about a city vibrant and alive. As I walked the streets of Jerusalem, I did not know the city. I didn't understand the language. Yet I never felt as a tourist. These were my people. I belonged here.

"One can't go to Jerusalem without visiting the Western Wall, the only thing left standing of King Solomon's temple. Some people call it the Wailing Wall. We Jews say simply, *Kotel*— the Wall. I touched the Wall, and the Wall touched my soul. My thoughts wandered between past and present.

"I have lived through the twentieth century, a period when many incredible events happened to my people in those short one hundred years. We went from Holocaust to New Life. From Auschwitz to a free Israel. I, little me, had witnessed it all. As a young girl I stood in Auschwitz in front of the crematorium, and now I am standing here in a free Israel, surrounded by my people in front of this most sacred place, so close to God. It was all mind-boggling. When I said good-bye to Israel, my heart filled with sadness. But I left part of myself there. I left my family there. And I know, I positively know, I will be back."

Helen at the Kotel, the Western Wall of the Temple in Jerusalem.

"What a powerful experience." My friend continued to amaze me.

"Yes, and while this was a good dream come true, I also had a bad dream come true while there."

"Oh, what happened?"

"Before we had left home, I had been telling my psychologist that I had a dream that I got lost and I went from one place to another place and every time I came to a corner I said to myself, now I know where I am, I just have to turn right. He told me people often dream they get lost. Well, while I was at the Wall, I wandered off and got lost in what's referred to as *Old Jerusalem.*"

"By yourself?"

"By myself. And if you would see all of Old Jerusalem, you would know what I am talking about. I went from street to street thousands of years old, all empty. The buildings were empty! No one lives there. There are some buildings people study in, but for Shabbat they were empty. I kept thinking, at the end of the street I will know where I am. But I got in deeper and deeper. You see, that's very dangerous because the streets are open to the Arabs too, so they could kidnap someone or whatever. This was 1992. I went from street to street to street and getting deeper and deeper."

"Were you terrified?"

"It was exactly what I dreamed before. I am living my bad dream. After a while a group who happened to be from Tucson, and staying at a hotel near ours, noticed I was wearing one of our *Phoenix 100* jackets, approached me and spoke in English, 'You are from Phoenix, you have to come with us.' I didn't want to even notice them. They didn't exist for me; I wasn't going to go with them. But they practically dragged me with them and took me to the their hotel and called my hotel and said, 'One of your people is here and she doesn't even want to tell us her name, but she is from Phoenix.' And they said, 'Yes, that is Helen Handler and we were looking for her all over. After an hour we just left and we thought maybe she got a ride to back to our hotel.' So they came to pick me up and take me back. I was so embarrassed that all of the other ninety-nine people knew that I got lost in Jerusalem."

"The other group was from Tucson, but I'm still unclear why you didn't . . ."

"I don't know why. Because they didn't exist."

"It was just something in your head?"

"Yes," she said.

"Something in your psyche kept you from trusting them?"

"It's like I belonged there. I felt that if I go up the right street, I'll be home, in my home. I dreamt about it before."

"Were you fearful while you were going through this?"

"No."

"It was more of a seeking, a search."

"So were you almost disappointed when you had to leave?"

"I don't know. I was also very embarrassed."

"You are really operating out of two minds, Helen. There's the present tense in the modern day mind, and then you have this other mind that is so entrenched in . . ."

"I have the continual urge to go home. Do you know that for years, when I was frustrated, I uttered to myself in Hungarian, 'Mom, I want to go home.' It's like that would have solved my problem. Don't forget, before I was married I was alone on the American continent. Do you know what it means to be on another continent with other language, other customs, with other people, no connection whatsoever?"

"No. I do not," I answered. "When I turned forty I went to Ireland alone and that was huge for me, and here I was at the age of forty with three children. It was the grandest adventure of my life. After all, I had an upbringing where my mother's idea of a living room was, that is where you do your living. *Why would you want to go to Ireland? Why would you want to leave home?* But it was the best time. And that was nothing compared to you. Nothing! It was safe as can be; it was my language . . . so I can only try to imagine the enormity of your experience. You were young. You had no one to fall back on. It's just enormous!"

Helen just smiled and nodded.

A few minutes later, when I walked to the door to leave, she insisted I take her copy of *An American Tragedy*, by Theodore Dreiser, which explores the “blind blundering of the God responsible for complexes, suppression, hormones and vain dreams (H.L. Mencken).”

Oh, and some trail mix. Homework and sustenance.

Price of Survival

My time spent with Helen was forcing me to look deep within my beliefs. One area was politics. We disagreed about all things political, and while most of the time I tried to simply sit and be a good audience, plenty of times we went at it, practically throwing air punches in heated debate! With clenched fists raised, she would rail about current policies and trends until I would finally call a truce and we'd agree to disagree and do our best to leave politics on the shelf. Not easy, since all things are political. I felt that I needed to lighten our usual heavy agenda, so the next time arrived at Helen's to take my place on the floral sofa, I came in with a loaf of her favorite cinnamon bread—sans raisins—and a broad smile on my face.

"Helen, I am so glad to see you today. I've missed you! Before I get into questions, is there anything you particularly want to talk about today?"

"No, not really. As a matter of fact, I was going to ask you to ask me questions." She paused and looked as if in pain. Finally she lowered her voice to say, "You never know how depressed I can be before you come."

"Oh, I hope it's not because I'm coming."

"No, you bring life back into me and that's what people do even with their phone calls sometimes. But I hate myself because the place is not clean enough, it's not orderly enough and I always say I will do it the next day and I really don't care. I just would love to have it orderly. But I don't have the strength to do it; I don't feel like doing it because things tire me terribly. And I was going to ask you, how old is your mother?"

"She's eighty-six, but she's a very youthful, sharp, bright eighty-six."

"But she keeps her house clean and everything?"

"Yes, but she's like you now. She doesn't care as much. She used to be very particular and she's not now. It doesn't bother me, that's for sure."

"I was never that particular, but I always had a clean house and if it wasn't so orderly I used to push it in drawers."

"Oh, heck, me too! At least it can look orderly and we can fool everyone!" I said. We laughed.

"This is about the only room that is even half orderly. The bedroom where I spend most of my day is never orderly anymore." Then just like that, Helen has a way of turning a conversation. "The truth is, Valerie, every morning when I wake up, I'm sorry that I woke up. I am not afraid to die. But it is like the book I have from a Czech poet who died of tuberculosis before the Second World War when he was only twenty-four years old. I always remember the lines as he looks out the window and sees life go on; he, too, spent time in a sanatorium, and he writes, *I am not afraid of death. Death is part of this hard life. I am afraid of dying.* And you see, most people are afraid of dying. They don't know anything about death. It's the process of dying—to let go. I bought that book when I was in Czechoslovakia because I was in the same condition. And I still am in the same condition, in a way. I'm not very brave; I am afraid of dying. But I'm not afraid of death. No, I am not afraid of death; I really feel like this is it. It's like sleeping."

"There's no after?"

"No. But I am afraid of dying because it is something I never . . ." Her voice couldn't seem to go on.

"It's the great unknown," I offered.

"Yes. We were all given so much time and if we accomplish our purpose . . . your life can be full, even if you live to be twenty years old, while other people's lives can be empty even if they live to be a hundred. And that's why I speak. I'm supposed to do this; it is my purpose. This is why I survived," she paused, then added barely above a whisper, "where six million didn't."

With that, Helen got up and retrieved a book from her shelf: *What Christians Should Know About Jews and Judaism.* "Don't worry,

Valerie," she said, handing it to me, "I don't want you to convert; I just want you to understand my people."

"I'm not worried," I laughed. "Religions are having a tough time finding me these days, anyway."

"Well, you know, I'm not sure what answers can really be found in religion. And yet, our questions are everywhere. A recent commentator on the news, speaking on the state of the economy, was saying that some of the upper, upper wealthy say that they're hurting too. Another said, 'Well, they hurt on paper.' They do not hurt on a daily basis. It's all on paper. They won't feel it; they just see it."

I agreed. "In class I used to put on the board *Money is the root of all evil* and ask, 'How many of you have heard this before?' They've all heard it. 'What's wrong with this as I've written it?' One or two kids would know it was an incomplete phrase. The phrase from the Bible is 'The *love* of money is the root of all evil.' It is not the money itself that is good or bad; it's the love of it, one's attachment to it. A worship of it, or abuse of it. I think greed is very fascinating. I broaden the concept of greed to apply to an *excessive* love and indulgence and need for *anything*."

"And you see there are people who are just as greedy for fame," Helen added.

"That's what I mean. You can be greedy for anything, for someone's attention or time. No greed is good. What is good is a certain level of a need for money, but as soon as you say *greed* that means a dangerous excess for something and I don't know how that can be good or healthy."

Helen's eyes narrowed. "Hitler did not have greed for money. He was greedy for power. And he just didn't make people poor; both he and Stalin didn't just impoverish people. They took lives! Not just the through the Holocaust, but the whole war."

"So don't you think greed is tied to ego? Because you have to maintain your sense of self at all costs. It becomes survival. And that can lead to loss of control."

Helen leaned forward in her seat and I knew a big revelation was coming from the master teacher. "The greatest . . . the first commandment is *I am your God*. So maybe God is greedy," she smiled.

"Well, ya know," I answered, "who better to be, eh? I mean, if anyone deserves an ego, it's probably God." We both broke in laughter.

Helen got up and walked over to her pile of papers on her dining room table, looking for an article in the *Jewish News* on the Ten Commandments.

"You know," she said, "I don't know how you feel about it, but most of our discussions seem to be about religion."

"Oh, I've noticed. I find it interesting."

"I find it very interesting too, because first of all, ordinarily, I would never feel so free having conversations about this. Because after all, I grew up in an atmosphere where you tried to protect yourself. With you, I feel we are free to agree or disagree. That's why when I explain to you my point of view, or of Jews in general, I try to be respectful. As I told you, I always feel we are supposed to be the light of all nations and I know only one Jew who did it."

"I know, the one with the public relations agents," I smiled at her.

Whenever our talks drifted into religion, Helen became particularly intense, and I tried to imagine a day-to-day existence for her where living alone afforded her little outlet for demonstrating her intellect. I looked over at Pup and wondered how many one-sided arguments the little Bichon had heard and lost.

"Let me tell you," she went on as she shuffled through her papers, "every religion has to prove that they are right. In order to prove that, they have to explain that the others are wrong."

I leaned forward in my chair and added, "And isn't that a shame. Because there are more elements of commonalities between religions. I think the main differences in religions fall more in practice than in philosophies."

"Yes. But that was the reason why the world hated Jews because if they were right, you mean all of us were wrong? And it is very hard to give up the religion that made you who you are. Many things Catholics do in the church started with us; we stopped doing it because they were doing it. And why did we stop if it was a true practice for us? Why didn't we continue? Then we would have lost our own. We had to put a wall where it said, *if you go beyond that you are no longer Jewish.* So it was a P.R. job. But it came late," she chuckled. "But if you are open about it . . . I assure you that Islam does not want you to kill yourself or to kill other people, for children to blow themselves up. After all, they believe in one god and that's not why God created you. He doesn't want you dead. You don't serve Him anymore! He created you to serve in this world. You blow yourself up and other people, you don't serve God any more.

"It wasn't hatred; it was anger, because God created every human being. Why did He create people who seem to feel mighty and powerful, but their power does not come from knowledge, their power does not come from wisdom helping other people, their power comes from eliminating other human beings that *they* decide have no worth existing. It's not even that they have no worthwhile value; it is because these are people that made them feel lesser and the only way they know how to feel greater is by deciding to eliminate every human being who belongs to that group.

"We Jews are not different from any other people. The only thing is, for two thousand years we didn't have a country of our own, so in every country we were in, we had to find a way to survive and when you don't have freedom, you have to be smarter, you have to work harder, you have to look for more opportunities. We were originally an agricultural people; that's what every holiday is based on. So why did we turn to the money-lending business? Because that is all that was open to us! I don't have to go much further than myself. My husband and I entered this country with five dollars between us. We were *never* on public welfare."

I was willing to look ignorant again. "This might sound moronically naïve to ask, but for the sake of discussion, can you explain simply to me why Jews have been so targeted. What's the reason behind anti-Semitism?"

"Kids ask me that all the time in schools and I have a hard time explaining to them. The truth is very simple. I am sorry to say it, but if you Christians are right, then we must be wrong. If Christianity is the right religion and the only way you can get to heaven, then Judaism is wrong. And they are not willing to accept it!" She slammed her hand on her chair.

"But it is also the Muslim world."

"The same thing. Mohammed offered when he was in Jerusalem to become Muslim. Same way as the Christians do all the time! The Baptists, the Mormons, all the time! Why?" At this, Helen pounded her fist over and over. "What's wrong with us? It is the original religion! I can ask you the same question. Why do the Baptists say that we cannot go to heaven? Does that mean that Jesus isn't in heaven? After all, Jesus was never a Christian. He lived and died as a Jew. Since he never converted, does that mean he is not in heaven? Politically, it always worked. The funny thing is, the people who started the hating did it for their own good. They have to find a reason. But for the simple person, the first thing they said you do not have to be circumcised. And then slowly things . . ."

Helen's voice drifted off. She was clearly upset.

"We don't do many things that we used to that Christianity picked up because we realized we had to make a difference if we are going to survive. So they chose Sunday instead and call it Sabbath, but why is Sunday the Sabbath? There are Christians who celebrate Shabbat. They are the Jehovah's Witness and Seventh Day Adventists. So you know, religion was tied to politics. And we have a different politics when we came here than the Native Americans. If you take it totally apart, it becomes very dangerous because you think—so what's wrong with God that He just sits there and lets all this happen? You have to make a very big leap of faith to strongly believe in God."

"Or at least in a participating god. I don't think it's hard to believe in a creator but it might become harder to believe He is involved in our day-to-day intervention."

Helen said, "Yes. For example we have no problem believing in evolution. We don't believe we came from a monkey, but we have no problem believing it took millions of years. You know why? Because it does not say in Genesis how long a day was. So Jewish scientists say, well maybe it was a million years."

"Because the measure of a day was the sun, but the sun hadn't been created before we were attributing things to days, measurements . . ."

"The sun wasn't created the first day. God took the first day for Himself. Would you believe, in our religion, non-Jews have only six commandments. Only Jews have ten commandments because if you follow that God is one, you can't hurt another person, you're not supposed to cheat . . . compassionate to animals . . . to me . . . I don't follow the ten either," she laughed. "In some ways I do follow the ten. O.K., let's put it this way, the third commandment: I don't honor my mother and father because they are dead."

"But you do honor their memory."

"Well, yes, and I do honor them, and I honor old people. By now there aren't many older than me!" she laughed.

"My mother is," I laugh back.

"You know, Valerie, I am reading a book, *The Horse Whisperer*, by Nicholas Evans. And I just came across a quote which I must share with you." She rose from her chair and ambled over to her bookshelf, finding the book and its marked page quickly. "Yes, here it is," she said, handing me the book. "Read this."

> *All her life she had lived where she didn't belong. America wasn't her home. And nor, when she went there now, was England. [. . .] She was rootless, tribe-less, adrift.*
>
> *Once this had been her greatest strength. [. . .] She could seamlessly adapt, insinuate herself into any group, any culture or situation. [. . .]*
>
> *[. . .] Having lost all connection with herself, she had lost it too with her child and, for this, she was consumed with guilt. (p.1178)*

Helen looked sad. "As I read this, I felt these words really describe me. This amazed me how much this is me. I was successful, but it meant sometimes to me very little because there were times I didn't feel I was successful as a single mother. And that was the most important part."

"I understand. We can feel we are so capable in our lives, but we will always come up to one area where *I have no idea what to do*. And we single moms never feel adequate, I suspect; the responsibilities are just too great."

"But the character in the novel found an answer and I really didn't. I went through eight countries and learned the languages in each. I survived in each. But nowhere was my home. That describes exactly where I am now. Last Saturday at Shabbat, I really felt sorry for myself. I don't know anyone, even among survivors, who is so totally alone as I am. They all have a sister or a brother. I have that cousin who has one daughter but her daughter has two children getting married now, so she had two grandchildren and her daughter is very close to her; they are really good close friends. She lives very close to her daughter; her daughter comes and sees her every day. You know, she has a family. So I was thinking, do I know anyone? I have friends but . . . I mean, who are mine? I have a son, but boys are not like that and especially he is not like that because in spite of everything, he, too, is alone. He is not married; he doesn't have any children. I often feel I can't call my married friends. They always say, yes you can come over, but that's not the way the husband feels. Do you know what I mean? And you can do that maybe once in a month or once a year. You can overdo that. Then I have women who don't have husbands, but who have grandchildren. So it's . . . I don't know absolutely anyone who is so totally alone. Pup. I have Pup."

"So what do you do when you get into that . . . place?"

"I cry. I cry for my mother." Helen's grief always returned to the mother. I felt woefully without skill or equipment or eloquence in quenching this thirst. She sat in silence, almost unable to form her words. Finally, she was able to continue. "You know I told you several times that as a child I imagined I was totally alone in the world and the people around me I only imagined and now I know it was because I truly was alone, because no one understood me and they didn't even try, because I came from a world where a child wasn't even capable of thinking that way. All you have to offer a child is a family and a home and food and shelter. So when I found myself in Auschwitz, on my own," her speech slowed, "it didn't seem so odd for me to be totally alone. And I knew that only if I concentrate on my own inner strength I might survive. And the people who saved me really weren't my friends. They just did a one time incredible deed and that saved me for that period; from this one situation that I wouldn't have been able to survive to the next day if I wouldn't have had the help from these people that I didn't know before that just had a chance to help me once. Does that make sense to you?"

"Yes."

"They put me from one situation to another situation, but it doesn't mean that they connected with me emotionally."

"They cared about you, but it's not that they loved you."

"That's right. And it wasn't a continuing situation. Next time when I came to a situation where it was absolutely impossible, someone else . . . and that's why there was no way I could not believe in God, because it wasn't the same person, it wasn't the same danger."

"It seemed divine?"

"Constantly. Constantly. Another situation and someone else . . ."

"So there was some divine providence going on."

Helen nodded. "Yes, yes. Now you see, this is something I can tell you. I cannot tell this to a group of people, such as a school, where I cannot turn my presentation into preaching. But the truth, as I see it, is that divine providence is how I survived in the most incredible situations. So I mustn't squander the gift I've been given."

We continued to talk for some time about the daily emotional pain Helen still endures from her time in the camps, and I began to wonder about the word *survivor*. She has indeed lived on—she has physically, literally endured, but in some ways her survivorship had left her frozen for eternity in that horrific time and place. The Holocaust did not kill Helen, but aspects of a normal, healthy life were forever exterminated.

I asked her, "Are there ways in which you have healed? Is there any part of you that has healed from this, or not?"

"Now it comes all back, every part of it. Earlier in my life, I just didn't have time to deal with it because of all my responsibilities."

"So you can go through the motions of being healed because you have to get through the day."

"If I wouldn't have talked to you in the school, the first time you saw me, you would have thought I was fine. I look all complete, normal for the world."

"But the truth is, left to your own private time, you can't ever be healed."

"No. I never healed, I think, since I was born. My mother took very good care of me. She did take very good care of all three of her children. But even after my father died, she tried to maintain a lifestyle that she couldn't sustain. We were no longer in the financial situation where she and my father had raised me. And, do you know, I did the same thing with Barry. I put him in a day school where all the other children were very wealthy. And that's why I gave him everything even if I didn't really have the means. But what I didn't realize, and maybe my mother didn't realize either, was that it's not right, because I felt out of place. When I picked him up from his exclusive private school, the mothers who came wore incredible clothes, drove incredible cars, and I had an old car. And I was older than them because it took me ten years to get pregnant. I think I missed my mother the most during the years I was raising Barry. A mother needs her mother. I never had the chance to ask her for her help and guidance and wisdom."

I could see our morning's visit was taking its toll and tried to lighten the atmosphere in the room. "Helen, what are your sources of pleasure in life? Do you have fun?"

"My husband used to accuse me that I didn't know how to enjoy little things in life."

"Do you think that's true?"

"Yes."

"Do you feel at all that because of what you went through, and others went through who didn't survive, that you should deny yourself that, that you are not entitled to enjoy or are incapable?"

"I feel I don't deserve it, yes. Anything I do for myself."

"Do you like music? Art?"

"Well, that's the problem. Yes, I used to love sentimental songs. Having music is helpful, and I will go to a concert. But I like melodies, soft melodies. So why don't I buy tapes? But I don't do anything about it."

"And why is that?"

"I don't know." She stopped and sat silent for a moment. Pup began to fidget in her lap and she continued. "Because I don't deserve it. I always loved books, I still do. I read a lot. The trouble is, I have a problem. No one knows that when I read, I can't read too long because I get sick to my stomach. I can read for fifteen or twenty minutes, then I have to put it down. And television, I used to like to watch television, but it's so empty now. There is so much violence."

Helen was clearly fatigued from our conversation. She became very still and I could see her body physically let down. Finally she said to me, "Valerie, before you go today, I wish to give you something."

"Helen, you give me something every time I am here."

"No, this is more important. I want you to be the keeper of some very important letters."

She had my attention.

"What are they?"

"They are from my lover, Georges. You remember me telling you about him?"

"Of course."

"Well, he wrote to me for decades, you know. The letters stopped coming about two years ago. I suppose he died. I don't know. But when I die, these letters will get lost, and I cannot bear that thought. Will you take them? That way, I'll feel like they are 'home.'"

"Of course, Helen. I would be honored."

"They are in French. I keep them in a box tucked away. Let me show you."

Leading me to a corner of her small bathroom, she pointed to a cabinet up high, then said, "You will have to stand on this," and reached for a little stepstool.

I stood on the stool, and peered into the dark back of the shelf.

"They are behind all those other things."

I pulled out a 10" x 10" dark blue stationary box.

"Yes, that's it!" she said.

I lifted the lid to find well over a hundred envelopes and became breathless, imagining each containing its own words of love and devotion, spanning a lifetime.

"Helen, are you sure you want me to have these?"

"Yes. It is very hard for me to part with them, but take them today before I change my mind. I never know how much time I have and I want them safely with you." She sat down on the end of her bed and looked very weary. And very, very small.

"Thank you. I will cherish them."

Georges. Always in the room. I began to wonder if her unrequited love was yet another penance of the survivor. Not out of religious differences, nor the responsibilities of a single parent, but from a denial of the self does she attempt and fail at balancing the scales. The guilt Helen felt in surviving was keeping joy and happiness out of reach.

I walked out her door and down her steps to my car, clutching an old box of love. Another gift from Helen.

The Children

"HELLO?"

"Helen, this is Valerie."

"Yes? Good morning, Valerie."

"Helen, I won't be able to come out this morning. My mother passed away about an hour ago."

"Oh. Oh, Valerie, I am so sorry."

"Thank you."

"I understand. We will talk later. Take good care of yourself."

"Thank you. I will."

I was just finishing dressing to leave for Helen's when my sister had called, frantic that my mother, now under hospice care at my sister's home, was near death. My mother had been diagnosed with lymphoma fifteen months earlier and was now losing her valiant fight for life. I sped to get there, only to arrive fifteen minutes after she died. Despite the chaos of the next few hours to follow, I gathered my thoughts enough to know I must call Helen so she wouldn't be worried about where I was.

I had long entertained hopes that Helen and my mother, Loretta, would meet. I pictured taking them to a lovely lunch and watching the two become fast friends. Two charming octogenarians, both wearing the badges of honor and survival earned by their generation, yet so very different in their own stories. Now, that would never be.

The next week I drove out to Helen's, needing to see her more than ever. She greeted me with an extra long embrace, cupped my face and said, "I am so, so sorry you lost your mother, Valerie," looking as if she might cry. "Would you like some coffee or tea?"

"Thank you, no."

"Valerie, I am sorry I could not attend your mother's service."

"Oh, Helen, I didn't expect you to."

"Well, it is just hard for me to get around these days and I really don't do funerals very well."

"That's perfectly fine."

"You know, we haven't talked much about this since your mother became so very sick, but life is very different when you get to be our age. Our bodies are breaking down. We can't hear as well, we can't see as well, we don't have much to do. It becomes harder to stay involved in life. Our purpose is leaving us. We simply get tired. Your mother was sick. She loved you. She never wanted to part from you. But I can tell you, she was ready."

I fought to keep my composure.

"Try to understand what I am telling you. It is very hard when you get as old as this."

I sat down on her sofa and took out the envelope I was carrying that held a photo of my mother I had brought to show her. "You never got to meet her, but I wanted you to see what she looked like. She was a beautiful woman, inside and out."

"Yes," she said, looking at the photo. "She has kind eyes . . . just like you. I am sorry I did not get the chance to know her."

Helen held my hands, her kind eyes looking particularly sad. She went easy on me that day. We talked about mothers and aging and children and love and death. I was aware, at every moment, of my extraordinary blessing in having had my mother for nearly fifty-eight years of my life. Helen lost hers after only fifteen. Fifteen. My mother saw her two children grow up, become educated, marry, have children and nurse her gently into her passing in the comfort of her daughter's home. Helen watched in terror as her mother went to the Left. She became a motherless child in an instant. She forever missed her mother's guidance as she raised her own child, and she was denied the familial honor of returning care back to her at life's end. And yet, as we two women sat in bonded silence in Helen's living room that day, I knew our one commonality; even at ages 82 and 57, we shared the ageless pain of being an orphan.

When I left that day, Helen gave me two butterscotch candies and a lovely scarf, green with small white shamrocks, which she had planned to give me for St. Patrick's Day in a few weeks. My Irish mother would have loved it.

The more time I spent with Helen, the more amazed I became at her resilience and drive. Despite her many aches and pains and fatigue of age, she worked tirelessly to involve herself with her world. Whether through volunteering with various Jewish organizations or speaking engagements, Helen was determined to make a difference. Many times I watched her take a phone call. *Hello? Yes. Yes, that's fine. I'll need transportation. O.K., I will see you then.* As many as four days a week, Helen dressed in a respectable outfit, patted Pup, and waited for her ride to a high school, or a rotary meeting, or a senior center, or a university campus or a synagogue or even a conference of FBI agents. She turned no one down. Her community, in turn, responded in reverence. I often gazed around her small living room at the gallery of gratitude expressed through plaques and trophies:

> *In honor of your outstanding service to the greater Phoenix community and humanity on behalf of the EVJCC Board a generous donation was made to send 35 under-privileged Israeli children to study the Holocaust at Yad Vashem . . .*

> *A tree has been planted in your honor. We appreciate your time and message of hope in memory of the 1.5 million children who lost their lives in the Holocaust . . .*

> *Yom HaShoah – your dedicated work on behalf of the Phoenix Holocaust Survivors Association for bringing knowledge of the Holocaust to students in our public schools . . .*

This accomplished woman felt no tinge of nervousness or insecurity while speaking. She walked comfortably among all sizes of groups and types of people, all ages, all races, all religions. To me, she appeared fearless. And yet, each of us, even Helen, has a demon or two that lies dormant until triggered. My friend's demon carried the name *Authority*. And it, too, had its origin in the Holocaust. The most ordinary situations could snap Helen's psyche back sixty plus years and render her terror-stricken once again. One morning when I arrived and stepped into her home, she greeted me as if mid-conversation. ". . . so I went to Walmart. As I was leaving the parking lot, I started to pull out because I saw someone was coming and a lady across from me saw a spot and just hurried and my car just bumped into her car. I didn't even see any damage to her car. But when she started to call the police, I left! I just had to drive away. Of course Barry later explained to me, 'Mom, that's a hit and run.'"

"Oh, Helen!"

"I prayed she didn't see my plates, but I do think it was her fault. Barry said, 'If the police come, do not say a single word. You say your son takes care of your legal things. You don't let them in, you don't open your garage to them.' After he said that, I was even more alarmed. I didn't sleep for nights. You know, this is what's terrible; people don't realize that, for me, a uniform and a policeman, well, at that moment I practically stopped breathing at the image. I ran! That is what I was used to doing! Barry always used to tell me that one day I will have an accident because when I see police, I automatically put my foot on my brake. *They are here to protect you.* I will never believe that. I know that what you know and what you feel are not the same. After sixty-five years I am just as afraid as the first day.

"Do you know, when I had my business I did my own payroll, I paid my own bills; it was a small store. I paid my monthly taxes. I did take care of all these things, but when there was a letter from the government or from the tax department, I never opened it; my accountant opened it. And sometimes it was nothing; in business you get that constantly. I still don't open an official letter. So you see, I really . . . I drive very defensively. It's just that I can't react like other normal people react. It's the same reason I have frozen bread in my freezer." She struggled to speak further. I sat quiet, waiting. "So I just wonder if normal people understand it—I am afraid for the rest of my life. Yet I handle it. It's amazing, I'm not afraid to speak to an auditorium of five hundred college students; it's just that . . . anyone in uniform . . ."

"Well, it comes from such a deep place inside that it really becomes an animal's instinct of survival."

"Yes. You know, when Barry watches football, he screams his head off at the players. Jumps up and down. The guy downstairs is mentally damaged; his mind is like a six-year old. And one weekend Barry was here watching football in his usual loud style, shouting at the television, 'You idiot! You just messed it up!' and my neighbor thought he was attacking me! He had called the police. I happened to be leaving my condo when I saw two policemen coming up our walk. One was a young policeman, blond, just like an SS officer, and he approached me and put his face practically in my face. 'What did he do to you?' he seemed to scream at me. The trouble was that now I couldn't even answer, I was so scared. Finally, Barry opened the door and they talked to him and I hurried down to my car and left."

The composite of the survivor was taking shape before my eyes. One who has no sense of home. One whose fear of authority permeates ordinary situations. One who is driven to justify her own survival. One who can never store enough bread.

Instead of my time listening to my friend's personal horrors becoming easier for me, it became more difficult. I found it coating my days. I was now completely steeped in the very subject I had long avoided. Somehow life had pulled me into what I had kept turning away from. One morning I tried to explain the depth of my emotional investment that up until now I had been successful in suppressing.

"Helen, this weekend I watched a movie on the Holocaust, or tried to, *Out of the Ashes,* and I couldn't get through it in one sitting. I was a tearful mess. And it made me realize that it's time I told you something. As we sit here and talk, week after week, I maintain my composure very well. I don't overreact, in part because I must stay focused and efficient in my task. I also do it out of sensitivity to you. I don't think you need overt emotionality from me. I know you don't want that from me, but I don't want you to think that it is from a lack of your life impacting me."

"If you can listen to it, then there is no lack whatsoever. It is a heart-breaking subject."

"*Out of the Ashes* is the story of a female gynecologist in Auschwitz. When she came to this country and sought citizenship and questions were raised about her participation with the Nazis and Mengele, her defense was that she had no choice. And now when I watch these films, they affect me even more because I picture you! I think of you and your family. Even just getting to the camps is the worse part, the cattle cars and arrival in Auschwitz." I couldn't go further. My voice choked.

"Valerie, I would like you to read a book, *QBVII,* by Leon Uris. In the book, the author wants you to make up your mind. If someone used people for experiments, it was a very cruel decision because he was making them . . . well, he was a German doctor, but when he came back he did feel guilty so he immigrated to England. And then he volunteered to go to one of the islands no one wanted to go to and be a doctor for many, many years, believing that if you do good, perhaps it wipes out what you did bad."

"A moral dilemma."

"Yes. So that's why this book is different. Another thing was that they knighted him in England after he came back because he dedicated many years of his life to living and saving people there. And he got married and he has a son and a Jewish journalist sued him."

"I remember the terrific movie of this. As I recall, he was suing them for slander. And the only way he could win was for him to prove that what they were saying about him wasn't true. The case shifted from being a judgment on the journalist to focusing on the doctor's own culpability. While the court found in his favor, technically, he was awarded the humiliating settlement of the equivalent of a dollar. 'My honor is only worth one pound.' And even his son walked out. So even though he won legally, he didn't win morally."

"That's right. But it's the whole subject while the trial goes on. I suggested it to my book club, but it never came up what the moral question was. All along, this is the fight: *Can you be forgiven if you use human beings?* He kept saying, 'But how many did I save? I killed so many, but how many more did I save?' But it doesn't work like that. The Jewish Torah says, if you kill one you have killed the whole world. If you save one man you have saved the whole world. They used to say six million Jews, including two million children. But they killed the whole generation after generation. How many Nobel prize winners, maybe we would already know how to heal all cancers, so this is the subject, much more than anything else. Can you repair?"

"So what do you think? Can you repair?"

"No," she said simply. "I tell you why, because the ones you saved you were supposed to save, the ones you took you weren't. You can't substitute one life for the other life."

"We've talked about heaven and hell and reincarnation. Do you think that those, like the Nazis, pay in the end? That after their lives there is some punishment or retribution?"

Helen answered in a measured tone. "They already paid here because they ceased to be human beings. Golda Meier said to the Arabs, 'I can forgive you, like the ones who killed themselves. What I cannot forgive you that you made killers from our children.' Can you imagine?"

"That's stealing someone else's soul."

"Yes. You taught our children to kill. That's what hurt her most. She mourned the children killed by the Arabs but she mourned even more that Jewish boys are out killing, and that's a very deep human thought. But she was deep. Everything is philosophy. What do I know?"

"Helen, is your God all-knowing?"

"Yes."

"Is your God all-powerful?"

"Yes."

"Is your God all-wise?"

Without any hesitation, she answered, "No!"

"Is He a loving God?"

"Is He loving when He didn't give me a grandchild? Is He loving when He puts one problem after another in front of me? Is He loving when I am stuck in this eighty-two-year-old body without the strength to finish another day? But still I don't deny Him!"

Helen suddenly looked very tired. I asked her if we should stop for the day, but she told me she must share one last thought on what drives her life's purpose.

"These things seem to come to me through my dreams. I've never forgotten a particular dream I had: I was on trial and when I walked in I was totally naked and there were the people who were watching me. I didn't see the people; all I saw were their eyes on me, like that girl's. Hundreds of eyes looking at me and I knew I am naked and I knew they were not. And I was screaming, 'I didn't hurt anyone!' I didn't do anything wrong, yet I would wake up screaming. And I used to have that dream for a long time."

Helen was now almost muttering to herself. For a moment I thought that she was completely unaware that I was in the room. But on she spoke. "For years I had a dream set on Fifth Avenue in Scottsdale. I find myself on the street of beautiful, high-end shops there and it's funny because Barry is with me, but he goes to look for our car to go home and I go to look for our car and the street is lined with antique shops, but the windows are full of furniture from my home as a child —*our* living room furniture. And I say, 'My goodness, how did it get here?' And I open the door and go in and my three aunts and my mother are there and they have chairs and thin boxes, like for tables and tablecloths, and they are wiping them and putting them aside, and I go over to my mother and I say, 'How come that I am out there and not in here with you? How come that you never bothered to take me with you? Didn't you love me as much as my little brothers?' And my mother puts down the box on the counter. And she says, 'We were told that one person from our family can be staying alive. We had one token, so to speak. And we sat at a Shabbat table and voted and everyone voted on you. So YOU have to get out of here!' And when I go out, the whole place is like a desert. I can't see anything or anyone and I go out in the middle of here and I think, 'I am alone in this whole world.' That's when I wake up. So you see, it's a really funny thing because I always feel that they let me down that I lived. They didn't take me."

"And yet the message in your dream is telling you that it's placing a privilege on you, from their perspective."

"That's quite a privilege!" she barked in bitterness.

"But you are the keeper of the family. That's both a burden and a privilege, and it's a . . . it's a gift."

"Is it?" Her face took on a hardened look as she suddenly rose from her chair and walked over to her bookshelf. "I have told you about the book club I belonged to for many years. We once read *Heart of Darkness* by Joseph Conrad. Do you know this novel?"

"Oh, yes, I used to teach it."

"Well, it struck such a deep, deep nerve in me and I knew I needed to write how this spoke to me, almost to save my own sanity," she said, as she reached for her copy of the book. Opening it, almost with reverence, she took out a folded piece of yellow, legal-sized paper in her handwriting, and handed it to me. "Usually, I tell you to read things on your own time, but I want you to read this now. It really sums up my experience."

I sat forward in my chair and began to read silently. The room became eerily still; even Pup wasn't moving.

~ In Joseph Conrad's Heart of Darkness, the hero, Mr. Kurtz, is obeying in hopeless despair. His last words were a cry: "The horror! The horror!"

This is how I feel about my own experience in the Holocaust. The horror of it is not only my own pain and suffering; somehow one has at least a certain control of one's own pain. The horror of it is the suffering that one is surrounded with. Horror and suffering wherever I look, all that horror and suffering that I am closed in with, that only multiplies my own. The fear and sheer naked terror in the faces, in the eyes looking into the barrel of a soldier's rifle, standing in front of the gates of a crematory or in front of rope, ready to be hanged. I have never, never seen anything even close to it, never before or after.

Inevitably, sooner or later, someone will ask me, 'Did your faith in God save you?' I can read it in their eyes. They want me to reassure them in their faith, they want me to tell them, that their almighty, merciful god came through for me. They seem to me so naïve, so innocent. What can I tell them? The truth is brutal, the truth is not noble and has little to do with a merciful, all-loving god.

> *How did I survive? By losing every noble, human quality one by one. As the horror intensified, the human quality disappeared. I survived by becoming an animal. I was treated as one and became one. No thinking, no feeling. I lived by instinct, only by instinct. It is so dark, so hopeless, so useless, so tragic.*

I looked up from my reading to see Helen searching my face for understanding, or at least compassion.

"Oh, Helen," was all I could say. I felt puny. I thought I knew her story, but the layers continued to fall away.

"Yes. Why me? This is the question I ask myself for the last forty-three years: Why? Why have I survived? I never feel that I am entitled to be in this world. It was not fair that I, just me alone of my family, survived. It was indecent, disloyal. I began to feel I must have cheated or betrayed everyone who didn't make it. I always feel that for this little place that I take up in air and everything, I have to pay back; I have to earn it. My life did not belong to me, so I had to do something worthwhile to justify my existence. What can I do to pay back?"

I set down the long, yellow paper and offered, "Can you see that you are doing that through your speaking?"

"That's why I am doing that. And that's why, when my doctor says I can't do as much as I used to, I tell him I have to do it as long as I breathe. I must speak for my whole family. And maybe that's why I continue to have that dream."

"Helen, I must tell you that at our Yom HaShoah ceremony, I pictured every one of them when you walked in with your candle. I felt I knew them. You have kept them alive through your work. You are the keeper. Like your dream in the antique store where you are being told by your family, *you are the one who is chosen*, like it or not."

"Yes. This is very much my role; it became my role in life." Then Helen's voice became softer. "But, I'm no hero. I never saved anyone but myself. And that was no big deal because I didn't exist, basically. That's the psychology of a survivor. After the war, I was still bleeding, but eventually a scab formed over it. No, there was no healing, but the scab became thicker and thicker as the years went by. Speaking to others became a help for me, a purpose. I am in another world when I speak. My audience becomes my world. They become my family and I have one hour with them and I have to save them."

That day's gift: a large cardboard box filled to the brim with a mere sampling of the hundreds of hand-written cards, letters, posters of thanks from schoolchildren who have been fortunate to "sit at the feet" of this wise woman with the story to tell that leaves its imprint on one's soul. Some were posted on construction paper decorated with hearts and flowers and stars and stamps. Others crudely handwritten on tiny slips of paper. Most reflected the awkwardness of a child's mind trying to grasp a very adult subject. Each message, despite most coming at the assigned guidance of their teacher, revealed the poignant, raw honesty of an innocent.

> *". . . I thank you for teaching us about the life you had and the things you saw during this disgrace that happened."*
>
> *". . . I just want you to know that you are honored by me."*
>
> *"Mrs. Handler, when I get older I will tell my children everything about the Holocaust and your story."*
>
> *". . . You inspire me because even though times were hard you never gave up. Meeting and getting to talk to you is the greatest thing that has happened to me."*
>
> *". . . Ms. Helen don't worry please just don't worry 'cause one day you, Ms. Helen, also everyone, will see each other again."*
>
> *". . . You have changed the way I think about life."*
>
> *". . . You made me appreciate life more because now we have the freedom that you didn't have. You and your story really touched me so deep. I will never forget about this. And when I grow up and have my children know about this so they can know how lucky they are."*
>
> *". . . My great grandpa fought in WWII but now I understand it differently."*
>
> *". . . If you hadn't gone through the horror you wouldn't*

have been able to share your experiences with us."

". . . You are a really brave woman and I never had a hero before but you are my hero, Mrs. Helen Handler."

". . . You have touched me in a way I have never been touched before. You are my hero and friend. I appreciate that you don't hate other humans. I also want to thank God for letting you live to tell your story."

". . . Your story made me cry, but I will use your lessons to be a better person."

"I will do my best to make it a better future."

"When you are feeling totally down in the dumps just look at this drawing of a flower I drew up for you; it's a lily."

". . . I wich I could of done something about it but I still wasent born yet."

The children. It was all about the children, she often told me, more than teachers' thank-yous or bouquets of flowers or plaques on her walls. "You are all my gr-r-r-randchildren," she'd always say to the one student who inevitably would ask if she had any. The softest spot in her heart remained reserved for those outcasts like herself. "When I am speaking to a class, up comes a kid who has a ring in the nose, two on the ears, a little beard, and he puts his arm around me, I hug him. I think he needs more of a hug than the kid who is just clean and all. I always try to hug a boy before a girl for the simple reason that it is much harder for a boy to decide to come up for a hug. I always try to hug a black kid, or a Hispanic, or a fat girl, or the one who is different."

"Ah, yes, those 'others' who are in every class."

"Yes. And when I hug them, I'm left a little warmer, because for the rest of my life I will always feel a terrible need for what wasn't there."

"And you let them know that you mean this."

"Yes. When they stand in line for a hug, it's fun. They laugh. They are young. So I hug them and give them even a kiss and I hope that they don't have swine flu!" she laughed. "And it doesn't matter how tired I get. Sometimes," she sighed, "they stand in such a long line and 'Can we take a picture?' Yes, yes, yes, yes. And they want autographs and my hand is shaking. That's the hardest part of speaking. It tires me out so."

"But it's probably also what gives you the greatest satisfaction, the most reward."

"Well . . . I think . . . I feel that . . . when after they listen to me and I give them a hug, that's like putting a stamp on a letter and sending it out to the world."

Reunion

HELEN HAD BEEN SUFFERING for some time with chronic pain to add to her host of other health problems, often telling me how badly she hurt all over. Her doctor finally diagnosed her with fibromyalgia. She cannot take most medications for various reasons. One makes her too groggy, while another makes her sick. Oddly, even her physical ailments seemed tied to her life's early damage. She once told me, "I feel exposed to the world in flesh, without my skin. All the hurt of the world touches my raw flesh, without the protection of the skin I am most of the time in horrible pain. I am hurting for everyone and for everything."

Her days could be catalogued into distinctive types. In one, she rode in the passenger seat of another's car to a school she had never been to before where she smiled warmly at students whose names she did not know, then plunged into her tale attached to messages of hope and love, leaving her exhausted, yet feeling purposeful. In another, she tended to a growing number of doctor visits for a growing number of health issues. Still other days were spent with way too much time on her hands . . . to think . . . and cry. And then there were Tuesdays with me.

On this morning when I arrived, Pup greeted me as usual. As I stepped into the apartment, Helen was standing quite a way inside, uncharacteristically passive and still. As I approached her, I noticed a large bruise on her left chin.

"Oh, my goodness, Helen, what happened?"

"I fell." Her voice was thin and hoarse.

"Oh, no! How?" I wrapped my arm around her as we sat down at her nearest dining room chairs.

"I was walking Pup. I walk a long way in the mornings with her, not just around the complex. I just lost my balance and went down to the curb. Well, I think it might be the medication I am on. But now my whole left side hurts so."

"Could you get home on your own?"

"Yes. I went to the doctor yesterday and nothing is broken. But I am so weak. So, you talk. How are your children?"

I spent the next few minutes talking about myself, something I wasn't used to doing. She seemed lost in thought, so I decided to just give her quiet, allowing her space to speak.

Finally she said, "I don't think I am going to be here much longer. I am so very weak. Everything just seemed to turn the corner a few weeks ago and I don't think I will ever recover. You know, in September I am going to be eighty-two years old. I've been lucky. I've never had cancer, a heart attack, a stroke. But I am so weak all over and hurt. I even lost my voice, can you tell? I was at a school last week addressing six hundred schoolchildren and early into my presentation I had to ask the teacher to have the children ask me questions because I could not go on in length."

She paused, staring down at the floor.

"I don't know. I just think I am not going to make it. So," she lifted her head, "ask me questions!"

"Helen, you have to know that I have enough material about your life already. I come now to see my friend."

"I used to have friends who looked after me, three friends. But now they all have lives of their own. Babies, grandchildren. One went back to school. I understand. But now, no one asks me over for dinner."

I leaned in and took her hand. "I'll have you for dinner, Helen."

She laughed, knowing that I live nearly an hour away and she doesn't drive.

"No, Valerie, that is not what I mean."

While holding her hand, I remarked, "Helen, your hands are so soft. How do you keep them so soft?"

"I don't do anything!" She laughed again.

For the next two hours we sat at her table as she drifted over many, many moments in her life, every anecdote I had heard, recorded, and transcribed. I nodded at times, gently interjecting, "Oh, yes, I remember that." But I never, never tried to rush her along. If she needed to tell this or that story again—for the twentieth time—so be it. She had earned it, God knows.

Midway through one of her tales, I was struck by an odd sensation of almost sitting on the ceiling and looking down at our conversation. I felt a strange freezing of the two of us. I realized what a vital gift the two years had been for me. And for her. She desperately needed to capture her life. To tell her whole life story, not just the oft-repeated Holocaust chapter. To have someone step into her home and give her two hours of undivided attention and companionship. And she was now so dear in my life. My friend.

But I knew her days were long and lonely. I knew she spent most of her days on her bed with Pup. I knew she lived for a school to call and invite her to speak. And I knew I could not be all things for her. I would never be able to fix her, solve her problems, repair the damage. It was not for me to make Helen happy. This was a realization that left me feeling empty.

I knew she was quite serious about the point she had reached in her life. Perhaps she'll live another three years. Perhaps ten. Maybe she'll feel much better in a few days. But I knew she was sincere in saying she felt she was fading away. It hurt my heart. Through all our deep conversations over these months, neither of us had cried. I recalled that recent morning when I tried to let her know that despite my control and seeming detachment as her "historian," I did indeed feel deeply about her experiences, as I started to give in to tears. But we both seemed to know that in order to get through all of this, we must not be blubbering women. So, despite the intensity of our meetings, we kept emotion down inside. But this morning it took all I had to fight back crying. She, too, struggled to stay composed. She encapsulated her whole life before my eyes, speaking again of her early loneliness in life.

"How do you handle that now? Have you learned to deal with it?" I asked, feeling pangs of fear that I may lose her.

"No. I sob. I sob like a child. Only Pup sees it. I am very, very depressed."

She abruptly folded her arms in her lap as if having just made a decision. "Valerie, I shouldn't have let you come today. It was very selfish of me to put you through this with all you have been going through. But I wanted to see you. When you are here, I am brought back to life. You bring me new energy."

"It's all right, Helen. I'm glad I am here. What can I do for you right now? Do you need any errands done, or to be taken anywhere, anything around your house?"

"No, I am fine. My refrigerator is full of food. Besides, I am not eating much. I can't."

"What about finding someone to walk the dog?"

"No, because the walking is good for me, too."

I felt so frustrated in not being able to do more for her, so I reverted to humor.

"You know, I took a bad fall myself last summer. Tom was coming in from the garage carrying too many cans of soda. One dropped and burst open, exploding cola all over our wood floor and our walls. I ran to get a towel, slipped in the soda, and went WHAM on the hard floor, blood running from my head. Tom rushed me to Urgent Care as my face swelled and turned variegated purple and blue. On our way home, Tom, in his problem-solving male voice reasoned, 'Well, I'm just glad I was here when it happened to take you to Urgent Care.' 'You nitwit, if you hadn't been there, it wouldn't have happened!'" Helen laughed and laughed like I'd never seen. "Good," I said, "My job here is done; I've made you laugh."

Two and a half hours later, I had to leave. On my way out, she gave me a small summer sausage, two kiwis and gourmet nut cookies left over from a Mother's Day gift basket from Barry's girlfriend, rationalizing, "Too sweet for me. You and Tom will like them."

"Thank you, love."

I left and drove away slowly, choking on my tears. I was tired of loss in this year. I had lost my mother, all her familiar things, her home to which I had always known I could run in times of need and find love and security. I had lost my faith. I didn't want to lose Helen, too. I couldn't even make it home. I pulled over to a little bakery to buy myself a lunch and be distracted by other people's lives. Then Led Zeppelin.

Guilty. I was still guilty. I have never seen what Helen has seen. I have never heard what Helen has heard. I have never smelled what Helen has smelled. My heart has never broken in the way Helen's has. For all these things, I sometimes felt guilty as I went through my ordinary days. Guess there was still more Catholic in me than I thought. But I was changing. Helen's courage in being willing to search deep within her soul to find her truth, and share it, pushed me to do the same. Why do I feel so guilty? Was I chosen to preserve Helen's story solely for her, or was I to find my own purpose in the journey? Was I willing to peel the layers of my own soul?

I did not agree with everything Helen said or believed regarding God and life. And many times I wanted to try to instill my own optimistic beliefs on her, yet knew better than to try. But Helen made me face my own concept of God. My hours and weeks and months in conversations with her finally made me realize that I continued to suppress the subject of the Holocaust's great inhumanity because I didn't want anyone or anything to tamper with my nice, neat catechismic compartments of faith. I had long dropped away from practicing my Catholicism, mostly due to my runaway intellect that could no longer embrace what I saw as an irrelevant and hypocritical organization. But I was still devoted to my own spirituality and relationship with my God. I didn't want anyone messing with that. Do not make me pull away the veil and see what I do not want to, or face questions I cannot answer. Allow me to stay in the warm, insulated cocoon of the universe I had created for myself.

Every day of her life, Helen's thoughts dwelled in the house of the Holocaust. I, however, had the luxury of diverting my attention, through my nicely-ordered, well-educated, middle-class, suburban existence. I had raised three wonderful children, found happiness in marrying my beloved, carved out a satisfying career. Why, before meeting Helen, I could go days without thinking about the Holocaust. Even years. She could not go a minute. Her faith was complicated. I thought mine was simple. It wasn't. Although in different realms,

Helen and I both ask, *Why me? Why did I survive? Why do I have to visit this reality?* We both feel guilt. We both wrestle with accepting the fact that the answers may not be coming, at least not in this life.

So, were my conversations with Helen expanding my faith or contracting it? What is faith unless challenged and re-examined?

I felt my veneer of composure thinning with each visit to Helen's. Any number of things we discussed could instantly move in a direction I couldn't handle. But there was one subject that I knew I must broach and it would not get easier by avoiding it. The next time I saw Helen, I sat her down and leaned close into her face before she could bring up any of her week's thoughts.

"Helen, I must tell you something, and it is very, very hard for me."

She sat still and patient. I could not go on. Finally, she said, softly, "Just say it, Valerie. What is it?"

My tongue still froze. Finally I spoke, barely above a whisper, "I cannot go to Auschwitz."

There. It's out. Now brace yourself.

"Helen, I just can't go there. I just cannot. I know many do. I have friends who have been there. And I know I should. But I also know my limits. This I cannot do. I would never make it. I physically wouldn't be able to take those steps. I'm sorry, I am so, so sorry. I know how important this is to you. I won't give you any excuses, just the truth of my failing. And it is a failing. I just cannot bear to be there." I was now bumbling through tears.

Helen took my hand in hers, leaned even closer in, and gave me the most compassionate of smiles. "Valerie, you don't have to go. You've already been there. You've already stood where I stood through listening to my every word all these months. You know more of Auschwitz than hundreds of visitors. It is O.K., I understand; you can't bear to be where my family lost their lives."

"No. It's that I cannot bear being where my dear friend suffered."

She squeezed my hand. "Thank you for telling me." And just like that we moved to the next topic. I felt enormous weight lifting from my shoulders. I had agonizingly deliberated this for months, and she wiped away my anguish in a moment.

Little did I know that I was soon to come into much closer contact with her world in Auschwitz than I could have ever imagined.

In the spring of 2012, after months of negotiations, complex arrangements, and risky physical maneuvering, the East Valley Jewish Community Center in Chandler, Arizona, managed to procure and transport one of six railcars presumed to be relics from the Holocaust, the type used to deliver Helen and her family to their fate. Journeying from exotic-sounding Macedonia to our suburban Phoenix valley, from its historical birth of 1918 to our contemporary 2012, the small boxcar was seen as the focal artifact bringing attention and, hopefully, funding to the group's planned Holocaust & Tolerance Museum. More than anything, it would start a conversation. Helen had long been a deeply revered, pivotal figure in the organization. As with her public speaking, she remained indefatigable in her efforts to see this museum to its fruition. One day she received a call letting her know that the railcar would arrive in four days. While it would not be available for the public until several days later, she was invited to be present when it was placed at its new home.

"Helen, are you sure you are up to this?" I asked.

"I don't know. But I know I must find out. Yes, I must be there."

And so, on a warm Sunday afternoon, Helen found herself standing in the physical presence of her past. She was grateful the public was not there. She was grateful that organizers were sensitive enough to allow her to have her own private "reunion," of sorts.

Helen is a fearless woman. Strong, and composed in her emotions when she has to be. But that day, her reserves fell away. It is one thing to own one's experience to tell others; it is another to come face-to-face with it sharing your same space. She stood staring at the railcar for several moments before taking the arm of her friend, Steve Tepper, executive director of the EVJCC. He helped her climb the dozen or so steps to enter the car.

When students hear Helen speak of her four days and four nights in this hellhole, one might imagine a much larger space. Measuring about 26' x 9', the structure defies reason. It challenges the imagination to envision fifty or more people—men, women, children, old, sick, pregnant, infant—crammed into the space of a modern kitchen.

Helen stood inside the wooden box and closed her eyes. In an instant, the old woman was a young girl—a frightened, naïve girl. To anyone else, the room was dead silent, but not to Helen. She could once again hear the wails of terror, the cries of physical anguish. She breathed deep and could smell the foulness of human confinement and deprivation, and the stench of fear. She could see her family huddled together, her mother repeating her mantra, "We must stay together, we must stay together." This tiny vessel of evil bulged with its memories of suffering, death, inhumanity, paled only by what was to follow. Helen slowly walked to one of the sides and tenderly placed both hands on the dry, rotted wood, stained with who-knows-what. She lightly ran her hands along the planks, as if allowing the very essence of her family to seep into her. Then she leaned her head, heavy with grief, onto the wall and wept.

Finally, after long minutes in silent reverence, Helen descended the stairs from the railcar and stood for a moment in one last prayer for the souls of her mother, two brothers, grandparents, and three aunts.

As Steve drove her home, she sat quiet, gripping her handbag for security.

"Are you all right?" he asked.

Exhausted with emotion, she barely uttered, "Yes."

When I saw Helen a couple of days later, she was still physically affected by the event. Her face was drawn and her body seemed to sag with the weight of sixty-eight years' sadness.

"It was a powerful day, Valerie. But a difficult one, a very, very difficult one. While I stood with my head against the rotted wall, I recited a Shema, a Hebrew prayer. It is the absolute basis of our religion. "*Hear, O Israel: the Lord is our God, the Lord is One.*" It is the prayer said when we are born and when we are buried. And it is what my people said standing in the gas chambers; that has been told to me by other prisoners who stood on the outside and repeated the prayer with them. *God is Israel. God is the One*."

My heart felt as if lodged in my stomach. I couldn't speak for a long moment. I finally said, "Helen, I worry about you. Did this offer you any resolution? Any peace at all?"

"No. Do you know why? Because I live with this every day of my life! It is within every breath I take."

"Was this a good thing then that you went, or not?"

"It does not matter if it was good or bad, Valerie. It is something I had to do. In some ways, standing in that railcar was a good experience, because as horrible as my time was in that box of death so long ago, it was the last time I spent with my family. I was back with my family for a moment. We were together again. We were reunited. Those four days were our last four days. They remain precious to me. It was what my mother wanted. The family was together."

That day, sitting in Helen's home, I finally cried in her presence. We cried together.

Helen Handler worked to help bring a Holocaust-era railcar from Eastern Europe to Arizona, a project that aims to preserve the memory of the Nazi-era atrocities. For Handler, those memories are personal. PAT SHANNAHAN/THE REPUBLIC

A photo of Helen reciting the Shema against the wall of the railcar, taken by Pat Shannahan for *The Arizona Republic.*

Dreams

Dreams. That nebulous never-land where the mind tries to work things out. Sometimes that is not to be. Helen continued to be tormented by her dreams. I came to visit her one morning and as I greeted her with my usual hug, she announced, "I must tell you about a dream I had this morning. It has left me very upset." I could see she was shaking, and I helped her walk to her customary seat.

"I dreamed about my father, which I never do. I somehow dreamt that my father came to visit us and I was fifty years old. I told him that I am fifty years old, but my two brothers were the same age as when they went into the camps."

"They're frozen in time for you."

"Yes, and my dream confused between my husband and my father. Anyway, my father promised that he would come more often and visit and we all loved him and forgave him for not being there. It was just so interesting. I mean, my father died in 1934. And I never, never once dreamt about him. I was six years old. When my father died I always dreamt that I was losing my mother and I was crying and crying in all my dreams and screaming that she was leaving us. That was because no one talked to me about what had happened. And I never saw him sick or dead." She paused, and then said, "This is something my father shares with my ex-husband. Both of them died away from me. I never knew what was happening. I never saw the event."

"And does that make it harder to have closure?"

"I don't think I ever had closures in my life," she answered.

I sat quiet, allowing her to gather thought.

"I keep thinking about my father and husband connection."

"What emotions were you having during the dream?"

"Well, this figure in my life who was my father, for the first time in my life I *really* loved him. You see, he was very absent in the few years I had him because he traveled a lot. When he was home, our household didn't go the way it went when he wasn't home. My father always brought gifts for us all; everyone loved him. But he was gone more than he was home. Then, when I was a little girl, after my father died, my grandfather was absolutely the most loved male in my life. He had a sense of humor, he was very loving, he was very giving of his emotion. You see, Valerie, even when I was at my father's grave many years ago, I was crying more about my mother that she was not with me there than for my father. I did want to put a plaque on his grave because I don't have any other graves. I did that."

Helen again tried to deconstruct her family dynamic. "For fathers who are gone a lot, it's an unnatural situation. The mothers have to establish their own rules and routine. From my perspective as a child, when I looked in the neighborhood where the husband was young and away at work so much, the mothers, and they were always stay-at-home mothers, and the children were having a great time during the day and when the husband came home, everything changed. Everything got ordered and cold and the father got all the respect and the children only talked when they were asked to. And that environment was created by the father."

"And you had that sense from your father?"

"I don't know."

"But you were in a different kind of household because the only male figure was a grandfather, which is very different from a father. Helen, it sounds like your dream is a very important one and it could be a major part of your personal well-being. I know I find tremendous wisdom in my dreams. I can work the metaphor out and get the message that I am supposed to get, whether it's coming from me, or God, or some other spirit. It sounds like this was a remarkable dream you had last night."

"That's why I was so shocked that for the first time I couldn't even walk Pup very long. I woke up and knew I had to walk her, but I just couldn't go as far as usual because I was still so shaken by my dream. I couldn't wash her up as I do. I didn't even make breakfast for her. I just wanted to go back to bed; I was so spent by it. I woke up very suddenly and I practically felt that this was real and they were alive."

I knew what she meant. "That's what I have found," I said. "When I dream of people very special to me who have died, and in my dreams they are alive again, it is so real. And it is such a gift because for a little while they essentially were alive again, they were right *here*. I don't wake up feeling sadder that they are actually gone; instead, I am grateful for those dreams, for the wonderful visit I just had with that person."

"Well, I never ever dreamt about my father. It's amazing that he came and he said, 'I will never do that again. I will take care of you, all three of you.' And my brothers loved him too. The little one was three years old. But my older brother, he somehow didn't stay in our house, but we loved him, and walked with him wherever he went. And in the dream he said, 'I won't stay away from you as long as I did, and I will come and visit you, and I will be supporting you. I will just be closer to you.'"

"So was that a comfort when you woke up, or did you feel sad?"

"It felt very good."

The following Sunday was Memorial Day. I rarely do anything celebratory on this holiday, such as attend a parade or other event. Unlike the patriotic hoopla of Independence Day, or the stars and stripes celebration of Veteran's Day, Memorial Day has always struck me as a time to give quiet, somber, reverent notice. I cannot "whoo-hoo" those who have fallen in serving our country. Theirs was the ultimate sacrifice, which all veterans stand ready to offer. So I simply spend some private time in prayer and gratitude. But this year was more meaningful to me. About five years earlier, my younger son, Greg, had a friend who was twenty years old, newly married, and the father of a brand new baby girl. Yet, he decided to join the Army. And this is what often perplexes me, that many who join the military are those who have people who most need them here! But he was hoping to finance his education; he wanted to be a pediatrician. His name was Nathan, a name he shared with my older son. He was shipped to Iraq and ten days later was killed when his army vehicle met with an I.E.D. It devastated Greg. So on this Sunday, he and I drove out to see the loving memorial that had just been erected in his honor in his small rural Arizona town. Locked arm and arm, we stood silent and still, both moved to tears.

My thoughts all that day kept alighting on young Nathan. And young Helen. And noble warriors and those for whom they fight and liberate all over the globe.

Two days later, when I arrived at Helen's home, she met me at the door and seemed to be particularly unsettled. As I set my things down, sat on the sofa and cued Pup to sit beside me for a petting, I asked her how she had been.

"This was a sad week for me. Memorial Day." She paused and stared at her fidgeting hands in her lap. "It feels like all these people died for me. A couple of weeks later, maybe even days, and I would have been dead. If the Allies had not joined the war effort for another two or three weeks, I wouldn't have made it. I am not for war. But of course, if the world had handled Hitler differently from the beginning, it wouldn't have happened. It didn't have to happen. It was just that they didn't want a war. Twenty years before they had a war that was supposed to be the last war of civilized people, which was very naïve of them, because if that was true, they should have made a different peace. By the time they decided to let Germany off, Hitler was already in there and what America did is try to tell them we will settle for less money, so when Germany lost the war, they had to pay for the damages. Well, they were in trouble to begin with; they really didn't have money to pay. But Hitler turned to their pride, and the whole world paid a very heavy price. But the truth is, I am always amazed as I watch these celebrations of Memorial Day, that politicians make speeches glorifying war, almost, and it makes me sick to my stomach to think of all the people who died."

I told Helen of the day's new sad significance for my son and me. "When I think of all the heroes who either died or were willing to, to save you and people like you, Helen, and those connections start coming together, particularly from WWII, I am overcome with gratitude for the depth of humanity."

"Yes. It makes me feel even more guilty when I see all those white crosses at Arlington or Normandy. And I think, all these young lives . .

. And in that war, these were not choices. It was *not* a choice. They had to go and once they were there they tried to survive. No one has the right to take away another person's life and today these kids volunteer. It's unbelievable to me."

We talked for some time more about war and sacrifice. And loss. Then out of my Pollyanna view of life, I once again sought to alleviate my friend's sorrow. I should have known by then that my single efforts would never be enough to smooth Helen's deeply-ingrained troubled waters, much as I yearned to.

"I've been learning a lot about how your Holocaust experience has shaped you into the person you are: your fear of authority, uniforms, government mail and how raw all of this can still be and your feelings of aloneness. I hope you won't be offended by the very notion of what I am about to ask you, but have there been any, dare I say, positive or constructive aspects to you that you think have helped form you because of that year and a half? Is this making sense?"

"Yes, but it is very hard for me to decide which part of my life made me who I am."

"That's understandable. We are all a composite of everything."

"You are right, because it wasn't a normal life at all. I know that when I lost my first home when my father died that I lost my security. I am never at home any place even if I own it. Secondly, I knew that I learned very early, maybe then, that to survive I cannot depend on anyone but myself, and that helped me to survive. As far as being influenced, I think that after the war, to rebuild my life taught me much more than in the camps because I had no control over my life there. It's not that I decided . . . I did make one or two decisions where my life totally depended on it, but it's not like my other decisions just helped me to survive my long-term situations. But the decisions I made after the war put me in a place that I could support myself and I could support my son in a lifestyle where only wealthy people could support their children." Her speech became slow and pensive. "But . . . I wonder if that was the right thing, because I never let him feel the hard reality of life. I never wanted him to discover how low one could go in life. Yet eventually, everyone discovers that for himself."

A long silence between us followed. Then she went on. "But Barry took away certain important things from home, from the way I raised him."

"Like what?"

"To answer you, I must go back. My mother didn't know how to live independently. My family used to belong to an upper middle class, so all my friends did, too. What's really funny is that I repeated this with Barry. My family placed me with friends that I wasn't financially able to take part in certain things that were very easy for them, and many times I was ashamed for the situation I was in. And while we were a group of five girls, I was the only girl who wasn't always able to participate after my father died. Even if my family tried very hard to make it possible, it didn't happen. And if I was sad about it, my mother reminded me that after all I was living off the compassion of my grandparents, and the situations were very embarrassing to me and it was really," she paused, ". . . you know, it happens in many families who have it well and then they lost everything, but the problem was that I was very sensitive. I don't know. I always analyze things. Do you know that I am a Virgo and we Virgos analyze things? Well, I am a one hundred percent Virgo; I analyze everything and maybe I would have been just accepting it. It wouldn't have made any difference with my friends but I never even tried. I was hiding my family's circumstances.

"I did the same thing for Barry. Barry went to school with kids whose parents were very wealthy; it was a very wealthy school. I had a discount and they always helped me to keep him there. But maybe I shouldn't have. Barry never knew that not everyone goes to college. It was always only a question to which college he would go."

"Does he understand these issues now that he is an adult? Does he appreciate the privileges he was given and by what sacrifice that came?"

"As an older person, yes, he does. But you don't get that easily over it when you are hurt as a child. Remember, he had that fight with his friend because I had an accent. Barry had everything, including water-skiing, everything, because there was always someone who loved him. And also, Barry was a Handler, and his father and everyone we knew always . . . He was proud of him but he didn't give him enough love. Why not? Because his father knew himself and he knew that Barry was exactly like him."

"His demons."

"Yes. Jack was just like Barry and Barry knows that he's like his father. Life is really very complicated."

"Like you."

"Well, my life never went in an accepted pattern. Any secure life I created came from my brain, not my emotions.

"But I am very proud of Barry. Today he is a respected, accomplished criminal defense attorney. In fact, I believe he was once named one of the 100 best trial lawyers in America. Of course I wish he were married with a barrel of grandchildren for me, but he is making something of his life. He defends the defenseless, a devotion he sees as a way to honor his people who didn't have that so many years ago."

Again, Helen's thinking seemed to drift off to some private, silent place, and I knew we had covered enough for one day. A few minutes later, as I was leaving, she brought out a necklace of beautifully handcrafted wood beads, made by Native Americans, given to her by Georges, her lover, when he visited the Grand Canyon, and handed them to me. "I want you to have these. By giving them to you I know they will be worn by a good woman." I had noticed by now that whenever Helen had spent time talking about the other men in her life—her father, grandfather, husband, son—she would find a way to resurrect the memory of her dear Georges.

The Mitzvah

I WAS NOW TEACHING education classes at a nearby community college. Each semester I drove out to Helen's to take her to speak to my cultural diversity class. I cannot count the number of times I have been privileged to hear Helen Handler speak. I knew every detail, every word, every nuance by now, yet each time I would stand in the back of a room and marvel at the transformative power of her voice.

But what happens when that voice begins to fade?

Helen developed a severe problem with hers. She had been maintaining a speaking schedule that would challenge the hardiest of speakers. Each presentation required more and more uncharacteristic stops to swallow hard and drink water. Her hoarseness grew. Doctors could not offer much diagnosis, other than to attribute it to age and overuse. They implored her to rest her voice, not appreciating that this is close to telling the woman to stop breathing. *But there are children out there who need to hear my story!*

"Why is God doing this to me? This is my life; this is all I have, all I live for!"

I began to worry for my friend. She continued to express a sense that she wouldn't last much longer on this earth. She wasn't eating much, and with her aches, her weakened voice, and now her anger and deep frustration fueled her depression. I tried to buoy her by reminding her of the inherent resilience and steadfast will to survive that has sustained her all her life.

She just said, "I always go through periods of depression."

"And how do you get out of it?"

"By being busy. I'm not depressed on mornings when I am going to speak."

Fortunately, this was near the end of the school year, and soon Helen would be summering in Portland, recovering her voice and strength. When she returned the next fall, her voice was a tad improved, enough that she was encouraged, and she was about to be reunited with the group that had started it all: Toastmasters.

Helen had not been an active member of Toastmasters for years, but she still held a warm fondness for all it stood for and all it offered others. So she was elated to learn they would be honoring her with a lifetime achievement award to be given at their semi-yearly conference held a hundred and twenty-five miles away in Prescott, Arizona. She called me asking if I would drive her there and be her guest.

"You will get a free lunch and mileage, Valerie. I could get someone else to take me, so I don't want you to do this just as a favor. But I would most want you to be there with me. Barry won't go; it's football season!"

"Sure, Helen, I'll drive you up there."

The following week we set out on our two-hour drive.

"Now, Valerie, I don't want to talk on the way up there, to save my voice."

"Of course, I understand." But I also knew what was realistic to expect. I'd been in this seat before. Helen talks. Period. And none of the talk is small; it is all sobering, philosophical, theological, analytical discourse. I just kept my eyes on the road and listened. And, most assuredly, learned.

Helen and I sat together at the table of honor. She is renowned in the Toastmasters organization, so many who recognized her stopped at our table to greet her. As I looked over at her now and then, she never wavered in bestowing grace and dignity to all who approached her.

Following an inspirational tribute to her, she slowly approached the podium to receive the District 3 Communication and Leadership Award, then delivered her trademark speech, adding, for the sake of her audience, the role Toastmasters had played in her speaking career. At its conclusion, the room was loud with standing applause. I just smiled from the side of the room, in awe of my friend once again. A line quickly formed to meet the little lady with the powerful presence.

Each seemed fully awed by witnessing history in the flesh. Some had their own stories of survival to share. Several knew someone who knew someone whose parents were liberated. One woman, about Helen's age, grabbed her hand, anxious to talk about her own rearing of five children alone in New York in the fifties. Helen touched all.

Many just said, "Thank you. Thank you." They didn't seem to know what else to say, except for the one older man who locked eyes closely with her and simply said, "Thank you for surviving," as if her very survival had somehow helped him. Perhaps it had. Then, making our painstakingly slow shuffle back to my car, we passed a man I recognized from the conference room. In a study of contrasts, the African-American, standing about 6'4" and weighing easily over three hundred pounds, looked right at diminutive Helen as we passed, and spoke to her in German. "What?" she turned and responded. He asked her if she spoke any German. "I've lost much of it," she politely answered, maintaining both their dignities at such a question.

Seeing how exhausted she was, I expected a long silent ride home. Instead, Helen found the energy to expound on the deeper intricacies of the Jewish religion and its current role in world politics. As a very excited Pup greeted both her girlfriends at the door, Helen asked me to wait for a moment. She left the room and returned with her copies of Chaim Potok's novels *The Chosen,* and *The Promise*, insisting that I read them because "then you will understand me, adding, "I've marked a page for you." She leaned close to me and gave me a kiss on the cheek.

I smiled. "Thanks, Helen. And thank you for the day."

"No, Valerie, thank you."

Whatever unoccupied space that was still left on my bookshelf was beginning to close in, but I was to later realize that that day Helen had given me perhaps her most valuable literary gift yet.

I sat down with Helen soon after and asked her why it was so important that she get her story told in print.

She replied with a tone of conviction that told me she had thought about this many, many times. And I knew to get comfortable, as it likely would not be a short answer.

"All my life after I was alone, I felt you have to fight for your life every day. You do not wait. You do not procrastinate. I want to live now. Now! And I am going to make it. I am going to find a way to make it. And someone will always be there to help me make it and someone always was. I want to be there for others in the only way I can. I don't want or need fame or money. I know my time on this earth is limited and perhaps short at this point. I don't even care if I am around when my story is printed. I just want my message to be preserved. It is about the future citizens of this world. I want the young people to know that they are here for a reason. That if they don't improve the world, the way the world is going, it is self-destructing. We are destroying the atmosphere, the vegetation, the animal life, and the human life. We . . . it's . . . some way it is . . . I use God because that's the best way to make sense of it. He created us perfect, Adam and Eve were in Paradise; everything was perfect. Everything that was in Paradise was created for human beings. If God is the way we imagine Him, He wouldn't take a whole week to create the world or He wouldn't take millions of years to create the world—whatever you believe in. We read in Genesis how God created light and then He saw that it was good. Well, if He is God, didn't He know that it was going to be good? Was he experimenting? Or was He sure that what He was creating is perfection?

"On the other hand," she continued, "we never created all this . . . if we lived millions of years, or thousands of years—Jews will tell you five thousand, but there were pagans before—we could never truly create something from nothing. Everything that science comes up with is created, connecting two or three different things. Things that came from God. The only medical phenomenon that is happening where we are practically even with God is when we make a baby, because out of an egg and out of a sperm grows a whole human being. But the first person didn't come from an egg and a sperm. It came from dust, and even after He created a person from dust, it was just dust. He actually had to share his breath with that form for that form to become a human being and even then the human being wasn't perfect, but still it wasn't perfect living alone because He had to create a woman." She laughed and added, "He didn't know the trouble He's getting into! There was

God, who created a fantastic perfect world and now a perfect human being. How come he needed a woman? It's very complicated, but in science every gas, every light, is here! We just needed to learn how to use it. So that means this world is totally perfect. And one day, the whole world may realize we pray to the same God. Then hate may not have a chance to grow over and over and over."

I sat marveling at the limitless intellectual energy before me. The elder teacher in the room went on. "So this is what we have to do: instead of worrying and going to the moon, make this place livable! And if we don't do it, it's not going to happen. The truth is, we are not doing it. The children are our hope, and when I look at them I think, *don't you understand how important you are*? Fun, enjoyment, and happiness comes from what you do, not necessarily from what other people do for you. *For the dead and the living, we must bear witness.* That is why I speak. I speak for the dead. I speak because I have to prove to God that He did not make a mistake in sparing my life. I ask the students to imagine being uprooted from their homes and being told to take only what fits into a small suitcase. I tell them it is their obligation to improve the world. I say to them, 'You don't want your children surrounded by hatred like I was.'"

Helen was now caught up in a purpose. "I tell all students that we didn't talk to our children about vengeance. We didn't put a gun in our children's hands and send them out to be killed. We put a book in our children's hands. Our children, more than eighty percent, are college graduates. We know how destructive hate is. There is no one who will know more than we did how destructive is the nature of evil.

"You know, Valerie, at one of the schools I spoke at recently, at the end of a long line of students waiting to greet me, a young man came up to me, twice my size and very black, not dark brown, and said to me, 'You touched my soul.' He then asked if he could sing for me, and right there he sang a hymn from his church. He had a voice that was incredible." Helen stopped, as if hearing the music in her head. She smiled with joy and said, "I am happy that that young man decided that the only thing he can give me is a song. This is why I do it. It is important for me to talk about it. It doesn't matter how hard it is. The giving of yourself is very important. You have to do things to show you are a part of this world. I do not take my existing, my surviving, my being here as a miracle; I look at it as an obligation."

"It is a mitzvah!"

"Yes," Helen laughed, amused by my newfound Hebrew she had earlier taught me. "Yes, a mitzvah."

I noted the lovely bouquet of fresh pink carnations that sat in a vase on her coffee table, a frequent gift of gratitude from teachers and their classes. Helen appeared slightly annoyed.

"I love flowers, but I wish I wouldn't get them after I have been speaking, because I feel I was there to give something, not receive. On the other hand, Rabbi Sherwin used to tell me, 'but it is also your obligation to give other people a chance to give to you because that's *their* need.' And he is right. When someone feels the need to give to another, they must. If you are a Jew, you have to, believe me, you have to learn this because this is what you are supposed to do."

"My Irish Catholic grandmother taught me the same thing. Whenever she'd give me a present I would gush, 'Oh, no, you don't have to, really, you needn't . . .' 'Valerie!' she'd admonish me, 'just say *Thanks, I'll take it*. Do not deny me the pleasure and blessing of giving to you.'"

"It's true; the mitzvah is a blessing to both. I remember asking a rabbi to come to do a funeral for someone who didn't have a rabbi, and when I thanked him he said, 'Helen, don't you dare to; you are taking away the mitzvah that I just gave.'"

"It is hard for some people to receive."

"And do you know why? Because they still want the pleasure that they still give and you owe them something. It's a selfish thing."

I answered, "Oh my, I never quite reduced it to a selfish act. But in a way, you are right. I have trouble accepting compliments. I have a bad habit of eroding their words saying things like 'Oh, this old thing,' or just giving them body language that I am uncomfortable by their kind words."

Helen nodded and said, "I have a hard time with it when people say *thank you* for speaking. I usually say, 'Well that's what I am supposed to do.'"

As I left that day, we stood at her door and Helen took my hand in hers. "You know, Valerie," she spoke in serious deliberation, "You have brought life into this home. You brought energy and a caring heart. You listened to me. So many others, including many teachers, wanted to write my story. But they were not right for it. I knew when I went to your class that day that you were the one. We made a connection."

"But I didn't seek this, Helen."

"I know, yet you did it. I knew you were sincere about this early on. After all, a person would have to be crazy to drive so far almost every week, and I've never even given you gas money. You have asked nothing in return. You did more for me than you will ever know. You gave me something to look forward to on our Tuesdays."

I stood there, just staring into those warm, brown eyes, unwilling to break her transfixed gaze.

"And Valerie, if everything goes away tomorrow, if you and I are no longer here, if these visits end for any reason, the truth will be that we were very good *friends*. We were good for each other. And every Tuesday we spent together was a gift."

The Chosen

I WOKE UP EARLY the next morning in a nervous state. I lay in bed, fixating on a dream I had, one I just couldn't shake. I was sitting in a teachers' meeting. As we all got up to leave and walked out into the hall, suddenly a very small, snowy-white owl came flying toward me. It latched onto the buttons of my blouse and held tight. I was startled, yet not frightened. After all, it wasn't an albatross, rather a beautiful bird. The owl and I began to walk a bit and it just held on to me, clinging to the fabric of my shirt, so closely that I looked down at it and could see its eyelashes. I just didn't know what to make of this. My thought was, *Wow, this is an extraordinary, exotic animal. I don't know why it has attached itself to me, out of all the others in the group. But it has. It chose me. How remarkable. I must honor that by letting it stay attached to me as long as it wishes.*

Thoughts of the dream lingered in my mind all day. Later that afternoon, I began reading a novel, *Zorro*, by one of my favorite authors, Isabelle Allende, in which a character was introduced named White Owl, a shaman with great powers and wisdom. *Hmmm, how strange,* I thought. And how prescient that made my dream. Or was there more to it?

As I related the dream to my daughter, Jenna, on the phone that night, she listened closely, and giggled when I related the coincidence to the book I was reading. Yet, even as I put the dream into words, I knew, I just knew the dream's true meaning. And so did she, as she declared, "Mom, the owl is Helen." Of course.

Helen is the small, wise, white owl who attached herself to me, and oh, I am so much the better for it. When I started my journey with Helen, I waded into dark, murky waters, fully equipped with insecurities. *Can I sit quietly in the intimate setting of a tiny condominium and bear to hear of the horrors of Auschwitz from one who lived it? Can I? What if I cry uncontrollably? What if I have to leave? What if I cannot do this? What if I fail Helen? Why am I doing this when I don't have to?* Yet, somehow, each day that I sat there, I was divinely coated with an invisible armor of resolve. I was not detached. I was not unfeeling. But I believe I built steel girders around myself because if I allowed the deep horrors and grief of Helen's experiences to gather like sludge at my feet, rising to reach my heart and mind, I would begin to sink in its quicksand. Then I would not be able to get the job done. I began to realize that the formidable framework was not shielding me from her realities, but galvanizing me to lead my own life with strength and wisdom. I knew I was in the company of an extraordinary soul who had much to teach me. And the world.

She often reminds me, "I am complicated, Valerie." That, she is. But one aspect to her that is not so complicated is the all-consuming drive to give back, to make sure that "God didn't make a mistake in sparing me." Through our years-long friendship and so many, many conversations, she has taught me about life from a perspective I never would have had otherwise. She taught this Catholic girl what it means to be a Jew. She forced me to examine my own faith. She showed me the importance of valuing traditions and holding on to one's core philosophies. She indirectly imbedded in me the reminder that I must keep in perspective every measly, miserable little discomfort or inconvenience in my day, and that I was equipped with all I need to survive when greater challenges would come my way. Nearly every day that I visited Helen, she would hand me something, large or small. She gave me candy and coffee, books and articles, lemon drops, and scarves and jewelry . . . and always something to think about. She gave me gentle hugs and held my hand when my mother died. She revealed to me the mystery of survival. She let me into her secrets and her love. Most of all, Helen gave me the gift of her precious time and memories.

During the next few days as I read *The Chosen*, I paid close attention to the page Helen had bookmarked for me, her telling me it is the key to understanding her.

Reuven, the young Jewish boy, is told by his father:

> *"So listen to what I am going to tell you . . . Human beings do not live forever, Reuven. We live less than the time it takes to blink an eye, if we measure our lives against eternity. So it may be asked what value is there to a human life. There is so much pain in the world. What does it mean to have to suffer so much if our lives are nothing more than the blink of an eye? . . . I learned a long time ago, Reuven, that a blink of an eye in itself is nothing. But the eye that blinks, that is something. A span of life is nothing. But the man who lives that span, he is something. He can fill that tiny span with meaning, so its quality is immeasurable though its quantity may be insignificant. Do you understand what I am saying? A man must fill his life with meaning; meaning is not automatically given to life. It is hard work to fill one's life with meaning. That I do not think you understand yet." (pp.217-18)*

I brought Helen to visit my class again. She walked slower than ever, her voice weaker than ever, but her brown eyes still sharp with the focus of one with a purpose. As I took my place on the side of the room, and watched my students' transfixed expressions, some learning of the atrocities of the Holocaust for the first time, I heard this woman of valor say in measured cadence, "Evil takes its victims, but it is self-destructive. Good people forever save the world."

Indeed, they do.

Helen and Pup in her home.

Afterword

I LEAVE THE LAST WORDS FOR HELEN:

In 1993, a few weeks after returning from my trip to Poland, Czech Republic, Hungary, Russia, Ukraine and then on to Israel, I wanted to write not only what I saw and how I felt, but how I apply that to what I see every day of my life back here in the United States.

Trees Grow – So Does Hatred

It was so green. The trees were tall and handsome. They surrounded me. There I sat in the middle of a field. A field in which stood thousands of people. Now they are no longer standing and no longer living. Rather, I was sitting under a tree, taking advantage of its shade, and knowing that underneath me are people who once stood here and died here for being no more than what I am—a human being.

Treblinka. One of the many concentration camps used during World War II in Hitler's plan to create his master race. I was there, not as a prisoner, but as a survivor. It disturbed me to see how well the Nazis covered up this camp. All the trees are the same height. They had, therefore, been planted at the same time. How could they even think that they could cover up this camp? Located among the surrounding trees were 17,000 stones, representing the 17,000 people who were killed here each day in this camp. This camp was just one of many.

The desire for a *master race* has not died with the passing of time. Just this past summer a group of white supremacists planned to kill Reverend Cecil Murray of the African Methodist Episcopalian Church, along with a well-known rabbi. Racism and prejudices are seen everywhere, even today. Could it be that we are turning the other cheek and allowing the white supremacists, skinheads, racists, and neo-Nazi groups to follow out their plans? The Nazis were able to follow out much of their plan to exterminate non-Aryan races. They knew that Treblinka was not efficient enough, but no one stopped them . . .

And so they built Auschwitz, another one that I stood in. It was also very green here, but the electric wire fences and the enormous red brick buildings engulfed all beauty. My friends and I, clutching each other's hands, walked through the gates of Auschwitz under those words that read ARBEIT MACHT FRIE – WORK MAKES FREEDOM. The B on Arbeit was upside down. The people in the camp who had made the sign wanted to show the outside world that something was wrong inside those gates. Work did not make freedom. There was something rotten going on in that camp. Why had no one noticed? Overlooking Auschwitz was a Catholic mission. Auschwitz was not far from nearby Polish towns. Could no one hear or see the atrocities being committed behind those gates? We walked through the gallows. We walked to the torture chambers. We walked through the gas chambers. We saw the crematorium. We were able to walk out of all of that alive. Others never walked out of it.

Today, the burning of crosses by the Ku Klux Klan is a vivid reminder of what the flames may have looked like coming from one of the main concentration camps. One cannot say that the flame of hatred has subsided. One needs only to look as close as their own city to see the smoke.

The Nazis collected everything from their prisoners. We saw piles and piles of old shoes, and artificial limbs that were once on people's bodies, and clothes, and luggage bags, and gold from people's teeth, and heaps of glasses. Then we saw the worst: bundles of hair. It surrounded us. Just as the trees in Treblinka had. Human hair. My hair was in a braid. I had been holding the braid when I saw other braids behind the glass window. But the braids I saw were different than mine. Mine had a body attached to it. These only had souls. I could not look at all that hair anymore. I ran outside of the building and began to write everything I was feeling.

> *Take my friends, take my mother, take my grandfather, take my brother, take my clothes, take my pictures, take my memories. But my hair. Why my hair? It is a part of me: Just as my hand or leg or heart is. I was born with my hair. It may not seem so bad that one does not have her hair. At least one could say to herself, "I am alive." But it is what the Nazis did with the hair—they used it to make clothes and to stuff pillows! They used a part of the human body in trivial luxuries. Then they would throw these bald, dehumanized prisoners into bunk beds made of wood and a sprinkling of straw. Six people in one bed. No blankets for the below freezing, snowy, December weather in Poland. Just their striped uniforms and caps on their bald heads, which did not keep them the least bit warm. It got even worse. These prisoners had only five seconds, twice a day, to use the bathrooms that were merely holes in the ground. And then the food. A stale piece of bread tasting like sawdust and every once-in-a-while there would be some watered-down soup or black coffee. That was a day's ration.*

I ceased from my writing, and then I began to think . . .

Today, this expelling of people belonging to another ethnic group is called "ethnic cleansing." The *Los Angeles Times* had juxtaposed two pictures, one taken in black and white during World War II of a concentration camp, and the other taken in color of Bosnian men held by Serbians in a prison camp. The resemblance was striking.

Auschwitz II is located a few minutes up the road from Auschwitz I. Everything here was left exactly the way it was after World War II. No museum showcases—just the raw truth. We walked into the camp by way of the same train tracks that had taken prisoners in by cattle car. This time I was no prisoner. I had not come in a cattle car smashed among all the other hungry, dying families. I was free to walk in and out of those gates. I chose to walk in. I stood in the same spot where the SS officers stood when a trainload of people would arrive, and could still hear, in my mind, the SS officer as he chose the destiny of arrivals. "Reh-khts. Link." Right. Left. One way led to the gas chambers, the other to a slow, torturous death of starvation, excessive work, and dehumanization. We walked on through the camp. There was a carriage like this used for to carry the rations of food to the prisoner barracks and then to carry the dead prisoners to the mass graves or crematorium. Then it was again used to take the food from the kitchen to the prisoners and on and on in a continuing circle of life and death. We walked through the rubble and ruin of the gas chambers that had been destroyed near the end of the war.

Some thoughts ran through my mind—was it good or not that some of these chambers had been destroyed and others had remained standing? The fact that many people do not believe anything like this happened during World War II led me to think that the buildings need to be left standing to prove the atrocities had occurred. However, what if something like this was to happen again? Could these same barracks be used for the same thing? Although I have faith in mankind, I often wonder if people would ever turn on others and cause such pain and suffering as the Holocaust had caused. The Germans had used innocent people as scapegoats, believing that they could solve their country's problems by eliminating them. The pain. The torture these innocent people went through. Why? Why was nothing done to help these human beings? One must think before pointing the finger at others. Hitler and the Nazis committed a terrible, unforgettable wrong. Today, people are using similar techniques to subordinate people and use them as scapegoats for some of their own problems. We must not let history continue in an ongoing cycle much like that of the carriage in Auschwitz II that carried life and death in it. One day, the whole world may realize we pray to the same God. Then hate may not have a chance to grow over and over and over.

Not many people had been able to go the way I was going . . . out. I am, in a way, "lucky" to be able to walk in and out of the gates of death, and survive. One would think that after all the death and destruction that I have seen, that I would have no faith in humankind. But for some reason, I do. I have my hair, and no one will ever take it away from me. I have, and always will have my dignity. Those are things I know. Like Anne Frank, I also know that people are really good at heart. I know that trees are not always as beautiful as they may seem to be. But at the same time I know that if one is living her life to the fullest, and working to prevent bigotry of all kinds, days will always be greener."

Suggested Reading

Night by Elie Wiesel

Day by Elie Wiesel

Man's Search for Meaning by Viktor Frankl

The Chosen by Chaim Potok

Helen and Valerie. Photo by Tom Foster.

VALERIE STAPLETON FOSTER taught high school English for thirty years and currently holds an adjunct faculty position at Chandler-Gilbert Community College in Arizona, teaching future teachers. Author of a memoir, *Dancing With a Demon*, and a short story, "Loss," published in the *River Poets Anthology*, she lives in Gilbert, Arizona with her husband, Tom, and welcomes conversations with her readers at *riskofsorrow@icloud.com*.

HELEN HANDLER is a long-standing member and past president of the Phoenix Holocaust Survivors Association and a member of Beth El Congregation and past president of the Jewish Free Loan. As a former business owner of a drapery shop in Phoenix's Metro-Center Mall, she is proud of having provided a livelihood for her loyal employees for thirteen years. Helen was a member of Toastmasters International for seventeen years and is a prominent public speaker in the greater Phoenix, Arizona area. A recipient of numerous awards and recognition, she devotes her time to speaking to schoolchildren every chance she gets, imparting her wisdom and message of hope and peace.

CPSIA information can be obtained at www.ICGtesting.com
Printed in the USA
LVOW05s2305081214

417813LV00026B/689/P

9 780615 978222